P9-DTU-361

THE CIVIL WAR

A PHOTOGRAPHIC HISTORY

THE CIVIL WAR

A PHOTOGRAPHIC HISTORY

STAN SCHINDLER

Crescent Books

New York

Copyright © 1991 Brompton Books Corporation

All rights reserved. No part of this publication
may be reproduced, stored in a retrieval system
or transmitted in any form by any means,
electronic, mechanical, photocopying or
otherwise, without first obtaining written
permission of the copyright owner.

This 1991 edition published by Crescent Books,
distributed by Outlet Book Company, Inc.,
a Random House Company,
225 Park Avenue South,
New York, New York 10003.

Produced by
Brompton Books Corporation
15 Sherwood Place,
Greenwich, CT 06830

ISBN 0-517-05418-3

8 7 6 5 4 3 2 1

Printed and bound in Hong Kong

Page 1: Horseplay in a Union camp.

Pages 2-3: The 1st Connecticut
Heavy Artillery at gun drill.

Pages 4-5: Union General George
Meade and staff.

Page 6: The 119th Pennsylvania
Infantry in camp.

Contents

Introduction

Today, while we are still adjusting to the idea of being able to watch television images of soldiers in action halfway around the globe, it is hard to accept that fully 130 years ago citizens of both the North and South were very well informed about the daily conduct of the Civil War. Journalists, artists, and photographers in the field made heroic efforts to enlighten the public as the conflict grew from limited to total war. Hundreds of correspondents submitted reports that conveyed the progress of battle. In fact, generals often found the newspapers more informative than their own field intelligence.

Photographers such as Mathew Brady and his frontline camera crews produced images of awesome intensity, despite the burdens of huge cameras, glass wet plates, and darkrooms rigged in folding tents or on horsedrawn wagons. The sketches and drawings of Alfred R. Waud, Winslow Homer, and other artists who traveled with the troops captured some of the glories and horrors, as well as the simple routines, of men at war. Publications such as *Harper's Weekly* printed engravings made from battlefield drawings; in calmer times – between engagements and after the war – artists painted watercolors and oils depicting their (sometimes fanciful) memories of combat. The demand for commemorative paintings of the war has continued into the twentieth century.

The thousands of photographic images recorded during the war were, however, available to only a relatively small part of the contemporary public. It would be almost a decade before newspapers and magazines would have the technology to reproduce photos for all to see. And the photos were static – slow film emulsions could not 'stop' action – but the images could be achingly clear. So, the mournful portraits, the blasted panoramas, and the volumes of pictures of the fallen dead capture much of the war's tragedy.

We hope that today, with our ability to acquire and reproduce visual materials of all kinds, we have created a meaningful evocation of the agonizing conflict that was the Civil War.

The Coming Storm

The Southern attack on Fort Sumter, the federal installation in Charleston (S.C.) harbor, was the immediate cause of the Civil War, but serious sectional differences between the North and South had existed since colonial times. The people of the manufacturing and commercial regions of the North believed that a strong central government was necessary to protect and encourage economic growth. The more agrarian South championed states' rights as a means of shielding themselves from such federal policies as protective tariffs, which increased the cost of manufactured goods to the South.

The South also opposed a national banking system, which it saw as jeopardising its demands for easy credit, and it generally resisted the building of roads and canals with federal funds. But above all, a quarrel over free public land in the West eventually made slavery the focus of all other sectional differences.

By 1800 the North was effectively free of slavery, but in the South, where the plantation economy depended on cheap black labor, slavery had become almost a permanent institution. When, in 1819, Missouri applied for admission to the Union as a slave state, a bitter debate erupted, temporarily resolved by the Missouri compromise (1820), which balanced Missouri's admission with that of Maine as a free state. But other stipulations left only two potential slave states in the remaining Louisiana Territory, and the South began to fear a steady weakening of its power within the Union.

By the middle of the century, the question of allowing slavery in the West had become the nation's most divisive political issue, particularly after the Southwest was acquired from Mexico. With Congress having to determine the slave status of the territories, men such as Henry Clay, John C. Calhoun, and Daniel Webster bent their efforts toward compromise, while impatient and dogmatic younger men such as William H. Seward declared in favor of a 'higher law' than the Constitution to exclude slavery from the newly acquired lands. Agreements, collectively known as the Compromise of 1850, were stitched together in Congress – California was to be admitted as a free state, New Mexico and Utah territories were created without reference to slavery, provisions were made for the return of fugitive slaves, and a prohibition was placed on transporting or selling slaves in the District of Columbia.

The issue, however, was not really settled and exploded again with the passage of the Kansas-Nebraska Act of 1854, which repealed the 1820 Compromise, split the Congress firmly along sectional lines, and roused proslave and free-state guerrillas to bloodshed in Kansas. In 'Bloody Kansas,' John Brown, an ardent abolitionist and leader of an antislavery band that included his four sons, attempted to 'cause a restraining fear' by murdering five proslavery men in 1856. He gained national notoriety and some support from Northern abolitionists who would themselves be discredited for a time by association with his failed raid on the federal arsenal at Harpers Ferry, Virginia, three years later. He had calculated this to raise a slave rebellion, and his attack did indeed cause fear of slave uprisings in the South. His sincerity and dignified conduct at his trial for treason left him a martyr to many in the North.

The abolitionists were heirs to a movement that had begun among Quakers in the American colonies. The more radical faction of the movement was led by New Englander William Lloyd Garrison, who began to publish his *Liberator* in 1831, and by Wendell Phillips, a frequent contributor. Moderates were led by Theodore Dwight Weld, a revivalist, and Arthur and Lewis Tappan, New York merchants. Together they founded in 1833 the American Anti-Slavery Society, which by 1840 included a strong women's rights group. Support for their cause was generated by antislavery literature, including Harriet Beecher Stowe's *Uncle Tom's Cabin* (1852) and the poems of John Greenleaf Whittier.

About 1830 the name "Underground Railroad" began to be used by slave owners for the system by which fugitive slaves were assisted in escaping to safe havens. Antislave workers adopted railroad terminology, so that 'conductors' – exemplified by the ex-slave Harriet Tubman – guided the fugitives to "stations" or "depots" where they were cared for by "agents" or "stationmasters." Southern attempts to enforce the fugitive slave laws only increased antislavery sentiment in the North. This was further exacerbated by a U.S. Supreme Court ruling (1857) on an appeal by Dred Scott (*Scott v. Sanford*), a slave who had been taken by his owner from Missouri, a slave state, to free Illinois and Wisconsin territory. Scott contended that his four-year residence in slave-free areas had changed his status. The Court decided that, as a black and a slave, Scott was not a U.S. citizen and could not sue in federal court. In adding that Congress had no authority to end slavery in the territories – effectively declaring the Missouri

Compromise unconstitutional – the Court stated that residence in any territory covered by the Compromise could not affect Scott's status.

A few years earlier a four-term Illinois legislator and lawyer named Abraham Lincoln, who had also served briefly in Congress, gained local prominence for speaking out against slavery. In 1854, during a campaign for Congress, when Illinois Senator Stephen A. Douglas proposed that Kansas and Nebraska territories be organized with no restrictions on slavery, Lincoln boldly denounced him. In 1856 various elements opposed to the Kansas-Nebraska Act drew together under the name Republicans. In the national convention that year John C. Frémont was their nominee for president, and Lincoln received enough votes to make him second choice for vice president. Two years later Lincoln was nominated to run for the Senate against Douglas. He accepted the nomination with a now-famous speech, declaring: 'A house divided against itself cannot stand. I believe this government cannot endure permanently half slave and half free.' The campaign that followed – highlighted by seven Lincoln-Douglas debates – attracted national attention and drew the philosophical lines for the impending Civil War. Lincoln lost a close election, but, continuing to speak out in opposition to the extension of slavery in the territories, he achieved a position of party leadership. In the Republican convention in 1860 he received the presidential nomination as Illinois' favorite son. With the Democrats split into proslavery and antislavery factions over the nomination of Douglas, Lincoln carried the election. Southern resentment led to quick action. Before Lincoln's inauguration seven Southern states (South Carolina, Mississippi, Florida, Georgia, Louisiana, Texas, Alabama) had seceded. Led by South Carolina, which declared the Union dissolved on December 20, 1860, they formed the Confederate States of America and named Jefferson Davis president.

In his inaugural address on March 4, 1861, Lincoln declared that on the basis of the Constitution the Union was unbroken and secession was legally void. A month later the Confederates fired on federal Fort Sumter in Charleston Harbor, commanded by Major Robert Anderson. The Confederate commander of Charleston, General P. G. T. Beauregard, had been ordered to prevent resupply of the fort, and when Lincoln authorized such an act, Beauregard opened fire from Fort Johnson early on the morning of April 12 after Anderson had refused a request to surrender. Two days later Anderson capitulated and evacuated the fort.

President Lincoln called for volunteers to put down the 'insurrection.' Four more Southern states (Virginia, North Carolina, Tennessee, and Arkansas) soon joined the Confederacy, but Lincoln was successful in holding the border states of Maryland, Kentucky, Delaware, and Missouri, as well as the western counties of Virginia.

Neither side was prepared for a protracted war, but Lincoln had overwhelming resources at his command – 22,000,000 people to the South's 9,000,000 (of whom more than one third were slaves); six times the number of factories and twelve times the industrial manpower; more than double the length of railroad track; and far greater supplies of essential raw materials. The North produced virtually all the nation's firearms, and Northern banks held 80 percent of the nation's bank deposits.

The Union army numbered only 16,000 men, most of them on the western frontier; the navy had less than 50 ships, scattered worldwide, many of them unfit. The South possessed no regular army and no navy, although some 230 naval officers – one sixth of the U.S. total – resigned to join the Confederacy.

Yet without doubt, the Confederacy possessed greater martial talent among its commanders, and its young men were generally more skilled in the use of arms. At first, volunteers came forward in great numbers in response to the calls of patriotism, adventure, and enlistment bounties. As the war drew on, however, each side found it necessary to enact conscription laws, the South in April 1862, the North a year later. The draft was unpopular on both sides, especially as the privileged were free to pay substitutes to take their places.

Almost 200 of the South's generals had resigned from the U.S. Army to join the Southern forces. These included Robert E. Lee, Joseph E. Johnston, Albert Sidney Johnston, James Longstreet, and John B. Hood. Others, such as Stonewall Jackson, returned from civilian life to service in the Confederate cause. Many were former West Point colleagues, and many had fought alongside each other, as well as alongside some of their Northern antagonists, in the Mexican War 15 years earlier. The Civil War would ultimately discover some great commanders, but at ruinous cost to both sides.

Opposite: The Hermitage, the home of President Andrew Jackson near Nashville, Tennessee. Rebuilt after a fire in 1834, it is an example of antebellum plantation architecture. For most plantation owners in the cotton belt, slavery was profitable, and although small farms outnumbered by far the large slave holdings, and although the vast majority of white Southerners had no direct contact with slavery, it became a way of life defended by virtually all Southern whites.

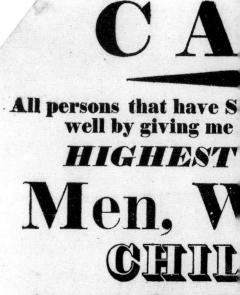

Above: A view of Charleston, S.C. during the Civil War. An important Atlantic seaport, the city prospered after 1800 with the introduction of cotton growing on a large scale. The completion of the South Carolina Railroad, a 136-mile link to the town of Hamburg on the Savannah River, allowed it to compete for dominance with its rival port of Savannah. Charleston was the site of the first ordinance of secession (December 20, 1860), and the war can be said to have begun here with the bombardment of Fort Sumter in Charleston harbor on April 12, 1860.

Right: A poster distributed by a slave dealer in Charleston, one of the South's notable slave markets. The first black slaves came to the city in 1672, and despite abolition of the slave trade in 1808, the sale of slaves continued as the demand for workers on the southern cotton plantations increased.

S H!

ES to dispose of, will do
, as I will give the

RICE FOR

men, &

REN.

ell, will call at Hill's ta-
me, and any informa-
tly attended to.

omas Griggs.
5.

THE FREE PRESS OFFICE, CHARLESTOWN.

Right: A slave pen in Alexandria, Virginia. The plantation system in that state had reached its zenith before the end of the 18th century, when tobacco was the principal cash crop. When cotton became 'king,' dealers in Virginia and Maryland were able to supply the new markets of the South; the slave population, less than 1 million in 1800, grew to more than 3.6 million by 1860. The building is shown guarded by Union soldiers. On the following page, the dungeon-like interior is seen.

Left: Cells in the interior of the Price, Birch, & Co. slave pens in Alexandria, Virginia. By the time of the Civil War, slaves had become extremely valuable; the auction price of a strong field hand approached $2000. Slaves were valued not only as labor but as commercial assets.

Above: The introduction in the 1790s of Eli Whitney's cotton gin caused an explosion in cotton planting. The world market took all the cotton the South could produce, and production doubled every decade until the war. As the plantations expanded, so did the demand for slaves to work them.

Left: Five generations of slaves on a plantation in Beaufort, S.C.

Below: A Currier & Ives print from 1883 depicts various field activities on a cotton plantation in Mississippi. It is impossible to generalize about the treatment of slaves in the South, but there is little doubt of their hatred for the system that held them in bondage.

Opposite: Springfield, Illinois, in the 1840s. Abraham Lincoln lived and practiced law here from 1837 until his inauguration as president. In Springfield's statehouse he gave his famous 'House Divided' speech. The city typified the resources available to the North. Located on a railroad in the corn belt, it shipped grain and had a growing coal mining industry and small manufacturers. Its population climbed from about 2500 in 1840 to 10,000 by 1860.

Above: Ironworks established by the industrialist Peter Cooper in Trenton, New Jersey, in 1847. It became one of the major producers in the United States, manufacturing everything from nails to wrought iron beams for fireproof structures. Such factories provided the strong underpinning of the Northern war effort, supplying arms the and equipment that were the economic base of the Union cause. The North had 110,000 factories.

Left: Edwin L. Drake (right) at the world's first drilled oil well in Titusville, Pennsylvania, in 1859. 'Drake's Folly' prompted the drilling of wells all over the world. The product was distilled to make lamp oil, and because of the demand, the railroads and ships that carried the product also grew and changed.

Below: Large, prosperous Northern farms, such as the one shown in this engraving of a settlement in Batavia, New York, provided a diversity of crops and a food surplus that gave the Union great advantages over the Confederacy, where cotton was the major commodity. A network of rail lines provided easy mobility.

Right: A view of crowded piers along Manhattan's South Street in the early nineteenth century gives some idea of the North's capacity to maintain its supply lines. The South had only a small number of merchant ships such as these.

ENUME of the in STATE of		
COUNTIE	Free white males	Free white females
Boone,	1679	1486
Cooper,	1612	1419
Callaway	712	642
Cole	532	444
Chariton,	583	541
Cape Girardeau	3526	3200
Franklin	880	853
Gasconade	650	463
Howard	3219	2690
Jefferson	875	749
Lincoln	823	636
Lillard	695	515
Montgomery	928	802
Madison	858	715
New madrid	1155	972
Pike	1286	1014
Perry	740	623
Ralls	742	581
Ray	912	732
St. Louis	3564	2858
St. Charles	1856	1453
St. Genevieve	1317	1081
Saline	519	476
Washington	1816	1363
Wayne	720	645
	32129	26903

*County divided.

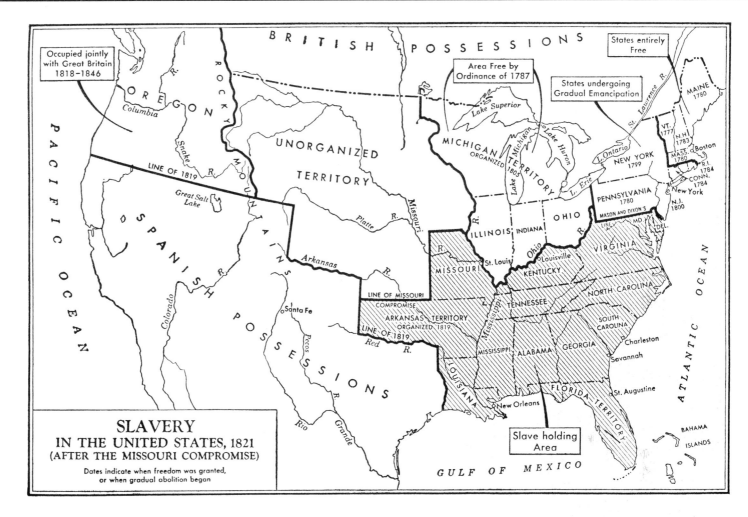

**SLAVERY
IN THE UNITED STATES, 1821
(AFTER THE MISSOURI COMPROMISE)**

Dates indicate when freedom was granted,
or when gradual abolition began

Occupied jointly with Great Britain 1818-1846

Area Free by Ordinance of 1787

States undergoing Gradual Emancipation

States entirely Free

Slave holding Area

Slaves	Persons bound to service for a term of years	Total	Representation
576		3692	3
440		3483	3
443		1797	1
52		1028	1
290	5	1426	1
1082		7852	6
186		1928	2
60		1174	1
1400	3	7321	5
200	1	1838	2
211	2	1674	1
180		1340	1
302		2032	2
344	3	1907	1
310		2444	2
425		2677	2
229	6	1590	1
358	2	1684	1
141	2	1782	2
1608	24	8190	5
738	5	4058	3
717	4	3181	2
178	1	1176	1
560		871	3
246	2	1614	1
11284	60	70647	54

ty of St. Francois 1

55

Opposite: An engraving of Henry Clay, principal author and sponsor of the Missouri Compromise, passed by the U.S. Congress in 1820 to end a crisis involving the extension of slavery in the territories.

Center: A record of the population of Missouri at the time of admission (1821) to the Union as a slave state. By the time of the Civil War, the slave population had increased more than tenfold.

Above: Slave and free states after the Missouri Compromise. By 1861 the slave bloc had added Texas. The free bloc had added Minnesota, Wisconsin, Kansas, Iowa, California and Oregon. The territories' status was at issue.

Below: Daniel Webster, committed to the preservation of the Union, was a strong supporter of the Compromise of 1850, which permitted expansion of slavery in the territories. For his stand, he was roundly attacked by abolitionists and by members of his own Whig party.

Right: The acquisition by the United States of new territories in the West enflamed the differences between North and South over the possible extension of slavery. This political cartoon published in 1844 attacks the attempts of outside forces to aggravate the situation.

DON QUIXOTTE:

„I bet Cuba!"

oy, you will beat them all!

JOHN BULL:
"I beț Canada!"

Below: Charles Sumner, U.S. senator from Massachusetts, was a strong antislavery voice in the Republican party. In 1856, after delivering a forceful address, he was brutally beaten on the Senate floor by South Carolina Representative Preston Brooks. It made Sumner a martyr in the North.

Below: Charles Sumner, U.S. senator from Massachusetts, was a strong antislavery voice in the Republican party. In 1856, after delivering a forceful address, he was brutally beaten on the Senate floor by South Carolina Representative Preston Brooks. It made Sumner a martyr in the North.

Right: Escaping slaves crossing the Delaware River on a ferry between Philadelphia and Camden, New Jersey.

Below right: William Lloyd Garrison, American abolitionist who, through his *Liberator*, published 1831-1865, stood uncompromisingly for an immediate and total end to slavery.

Below, far right: Frederick Douglass, the son of a slave woman and a white father, escaped from slavery in 1838 and became an effective spokesman for abolition. His newspaper, the *North Star*, and autobiography were notable for their great influence.

Below: A broadside advertising a public meeting to protest the Dred Scott decision.

Below right: Harriet Tubman, an escaped slave, became a 'conductor' on the Underground Railroad, leading more than 300 to freedom. In the war she served as a nurse and spy with Union forces in South Carolina.

Right: A slave shows his scars.

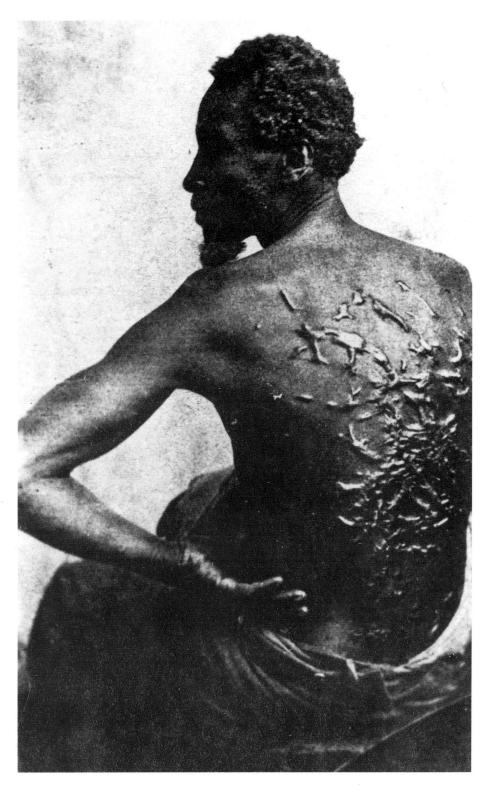

MEETING

ELD ON

, 2D INSTANT,

onsider the atrocious decision of the

T CASE,

eople are subject under the Constitu-

RT PURVIS,

ion. Mrs. MOTT, Mr. M'KIM and
invitations to be present.
tance free.

Opposite left: John Brown, a fanatic abolitionist, gained his reputation for violence in 1856 in Kansas, where he and his band hacked to death five proslavery settlers. This painting shows Brown in 1859 after his trial for the raid on Harpers Ferry.

Left: Colonel Edwin V. Sumner was commander of Fort Leavenworth in Kansas during the almost constant border war waged between proslavery and antislavery factions.

Above: A fanciful drawing in *Harper's Weekly* of John Brown's raiders on the way to the federal arsenal at Harpers Ferry, Virginia. The band, which easily seized the town on October 16, 1859, actually included only 13 whites and 5 blacks.

Left: The firehouse at Harpers Ferry where John Brown and his band, cut off by local militia, took their stand. The slave uprisings he had hoped for failed to materialize.

Below: Inside the firehouse Brown, his band, and a number of hostages await the assault on October 18 of Federal troops led by Lieutenant J. E. B. Stuart under the command of Colonel Robert E. Lee. Ten raiders died. Brown was hanged on December 2.

Below: Abraham Lincoln was licensed to practice law in Illinois in 1836. After two dissolved partnerships, Lincoln, in 1844, joined with young William H. Herndon, with whom he shared this office in Springfield.

Right: The Springfield law office from which the president-elect went to Washington on February 11, 1861.

Above: A highly successful lawyer and rising politician, Lincoln was 49 years old when he sat for this photograph. He is wearing the suit that he wore in court several hours earlier when he argued the acquittal of a 16-year-old on trial for murder. In two years, Lincoln would take office as president of the United States.

Opposite left: Stephen A. Douglas, photographed probably in the year he lost the presidential election to Lincoln (also the year of his death). The 'Little Giant,' barely five feet tall, received only 12 electoral votes to Lincoln's 180, mainly owing to a split in the Democratic party.

Left: The Republican presidential nominating convention in Chicago in May 1860. William H. Seward, the party leader, led after the first ballot, but by the end of the third ballot, Lincoln had the majority.

Below: The Republican party was organized in 1854. Two years later it held its first national convention at Lafayette Hall in Pittsburgh. Lincoln received 100 votes for the vice-presidential nomination (won by William L. Dayton of New Jersey). John C. Frémont became the party's presidential candidate.

FIRST REPUBLICAN CONVENTION HELD AT LAFAYETTE HALL, PITTSBURG, PA. FEB. 22ᴰ 1856.

Above: The last turbulent hours of the 35th Congress on March 3, 1859. The Democratic party was split over admitting Kansas, and the followers of Stephen A. Douglas opposed the administration.

Right: An Extra of the West Chester, Pennsylvania, *Chester County Times* extols the election of Lincoln as it reports the vote in the 1860 election.

CHESTER COUNTY TIM
EXTRA

WEST CHESTER, PA., NOVEMBER 7, 1860.

A Clean Sweep!

CORRUPTION ENDED!!

THE COUNTRY REDEEMED!

Secession is Rebuked!!!

LET THE TRAITORS RAVE!

LINCOLN'S ELECTED,

AND

WHO'S AFRAID?

PENNSYLVANIA,	60,000 majority.
NEW YORK,	40,000 "
OHIO,	40,000 "
INDIANA,	8,000 "
RHODE ISLAND,	5,000 "
CHESTER COUNTY,	3,000 "

VIRGINIA has gone for BELL.
NORTH CAROLINA has gone for BRECK'GE.

We hail with the breaking day the joyful news that ABRAHAM LINCOLN is elected President of the United States, and send it greeting to our fellow citizens! The reign of the Slave Oligarchy has ended, and corruption must cease. Let us rejoice as we read.

BY TELEGRAPH.

[Special Dispatches for Chester Co. Times.]
The returns from the interior of the State were procured by Mr. U. H. Painter, Superintendent of the Telegraph line.
PENNSYLVANIA.—Schuylkill county gives 1500 for Lincoln—a gain of 865 over Curtin. Snyder 650 for Lincoln.
Union gives 1100 for Lincoln.
Franklin county gives 1100 for Lincoln.
In Tyrone City—Blair county—Lincoln's majority is 25, a gain of 3 for the Fusionists,

Huntingdon Boro'—Lincoln gains Curtin.
Lancaster City gives 88 majority coln. There were 276 straight Doug.
Danville—Lincoln gains 78.
Dauphin county—1600 majority coln. Harrisburg gains 200 over vote.
Mount Joy Borough, gives Lincoln jority—a heavy gain.
Lancaster county 8000 for Lincoln
Allegheney county—10,000 for L
Berks county 1000 for Fusion— gain for the Republicans.
Westmoreland—100 to 150 for Li
Union county—437 maj for Linc
Centre county—500 majority for Brooklyn city, N. Y., gives 10,00 sion.

Philad'a, Nov. 6, 10.00 P. M.— more? here that Speaker Penning feated.

12.45 A. M.—The following dis just been received from Gov. Sew Auburn :—"I assert from reliable that Lincoln has carried the Sta York by 60,000 majority. Lincoln is conceded on all hands."

Philad's, Nov. 7, 1.30 P. M.—N City gives 28,194 against Lincoln. Messrs. Wood, King, Taylor and loco-focos, are elected to Congress York city. Eli Thayer is reported feated in Massachusetts by the re publican nominee.

LINCOLN'S ELECTION IS NOW DED BY ALL PARTIES.

2.00 A. M.—Philadelphia City giv m jority for "Old Abe"

CHESTER COUNTY.—We have only ships reported. They give Lincoln jority. The townships yet to hear swell this majority to 3000. The fo the Vote as far as heard from :

VOTE IN CHESTER CO. FOR PRE

TOWNSHIPS.	L.& H.	FUSION DO
Pocopson,	60	22
West Goshen,	101	40
East Goshen,	120	36
W. Chester–N.Ward	284	128
" " S.	220	91
Kennett Boro',	96	25
Kennett,	162	64
West Bradford,	195	71
E. Whiteland,	98	87
E. Caln,	122	40
Downingtown Bo.	93	72
Darlington's,	88	47
Birmingham,	47	31
W. Whiteland,	147	81
Phœnixville,	377	279
Schuylkill,	167	62
E. Marlborough,	218	61
Londongrove,	221	38
E. Bradford,	148	26
Wallace,	98	47
Upper Uwchlan,	81	82
Uwchlan,	104	55
E. Fallowfield,	175	97
Newlin,	109	24
W. Brandywine,	120	65
W. Pikeland,	57	131
Honeybrook,	218	137
E. Brandywine,	86	87
New London,	64	67

WIDE AWA

CHARLESTON MERCURY

EXTRA:

Passed unanimously at 1.15 o'clock, P. M. December 20th, 1860.

AN ORDINANCE

To dissolve the Union betwee ... State of South Carolina and other States united with her under the compact entitled "The Constitution of the United States of America."

We, the People of the State of South Carolina, in Convention assembled, do declare and ordain, and it is hereby declared and ordained,

That the Ordinance adopted by us in Convention, on the twenty-third day of May, in the year of our Lord one thousand seven hundred and eighty-eight, whereby the Constitution of the United States of America was ratified, and also, all Acts and parts of Acts of the General Assembly of this State, ratifying amendments of the said Constitution, are hereby repealed; and that the union now subsisting between South Carolina and other States, under the name of "The United States of America," is hereby dissolved.

THE UNION IS DISSOLVED!

Left: A handbill distributed by the Charleston *Mercury* announces the secession of South Carolina from the Union on December 20, 1860. By the following February, six other states will have followed, and this final split will have led to the Civil War.

Below: General Winfield Scott, hero of the Mexican War, commanded the U.S. Army from December 12, 1860 to November 1, 1861. A Southerner by birth, he remained loyal to the Union and is here shown fighting the 'Great Dragon of Secession.'

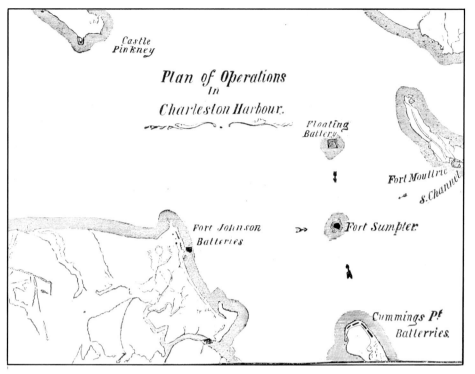

Plan of Operations in Charleston Harbour.

Opposite: In response to Lincoln's attempt to reprovision Fort Sumter, Southern batteries bombard the fort on April 12, 1861, signalling the opening of hostilities. Fort Sumter surrendered the next day.

Far Left: Private Edmund Ruffin, the Confederate soldier who fired the first shot against Fort Sumter.

Left: Plan of the siege operation in Charleston harbor, showing the location of Fort Sumter in relation to the attacking Southern batteries.

Below, far left: Confederate General P. G. T. Beauregard, 'ordered by the Government of the Confederate States of America to demand the evacuation of Fort Sumter,' informed the Union commander as to exactly when his harbor batteries would open fire.

Below left: Major Robert Anderson, after withstanding a withering bombardment, surrendered to Rebel officers. He and his men left the fort on April 14. There had been no loss of life during the engagement.

Left: Abraham Lincoln is inaugurated as the sixteenth president of the United States on March 4, 1861. A crowd of some 30,000 looks on.

Above: The Republican nominee on June 3, 1860.

Above: Jefferson Davis, president of the Confederate States of America.

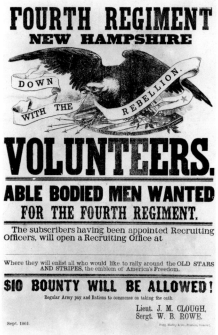

Left: Jefferson Davis is inaugurated on February 18, 1861, at the state capitol in Montgomery, Alabama.

Above: A call for Federal volunteers in September 1861. The defeat at the First Battle of Bull Run in July ended the Union myth of a short war.

Right: A fanciful painting of Yankee volunteers marching into Dixie.

Right below: A Rebel recruiting team parading through Woodstock, Virginia.

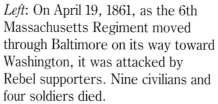

Left: On April 19, 1861, as the 6th Massachusetts Regiment moved through Baltimore on its way toward Washington, it was attacked by Rebel supporters. Nine civilians and four soldiers died.

Top: Zachary Taylor commanded Lee and Grant in the Mexican War.

Above left: Grant as a full general.

Above right: Portrait of Robert E. Lee as a U.S. Army captain.

Far left: Elmer E. Ellsworth, among the war's first victims, was a young Union Zouaves officer when he was shot while attempting to remove a Southern flag the day Union troops entered Virginia.

Left above: Major Thomas Jackson, later known as Stonewall Jackson, in a portrait made during the Mexican War.

Left: William Tecumseh Sherman as a young artillery officer.

Above: Alfred R. Waud, who would become one of the war's preeminent combat artists, sketched this scene of President Lincoln and General Winfield Scott reviewing a regiment on Pennsylvania Avenue in 1861.

Right: The storming of the Bishop's Palace by U.S. troops under Zachary Taylor in the battle for Monterey during the Mexican War. A number of young officers who together had their first battle experience in the war with Mexico would confront each other as commanders in the Civil War. Lee, Grant, and Stonewall Jackson were among them.

Early Battles and Campaigns (1861-1862)

By the early summer of 1861 small skirmishes and minor engagements had taken place, primarily in Virginia, where inexperienced Federal forces made probing thrusts. One notable attempt occurred in early June, when a small force of recruits under General Benjamin Butler left Fort Monroe to strike at Richmond. North Carolina infantry entrenched near Yorktown quickly drove them back. But by mid-July the cry of 'On to Richmond' was heard everywhere in the North, and, bending to political pressure, General Irvin McDowell marched from Washington with 30,000 troops to seize the Confederate capital. His short-term objective was the railroad junction at Manassas, some 30 miles south of Washington.

Forewarned, Confederate Generals P. G. T. Beauregard and Joseph E. Johnston massed an army of equal size. McDowell made contact with them on July 21 near a stream named Bull Run. Although close to success at one point, the Union force was routed by a Rebel counterattack after a determined stand by General Thomas J. Jackson (afterward called 'Stonewall') had bought time for Confederate reinforcements under E. Kirby Smith to arrive. This First Battle of Bull Run convinced many in the South that victory would quickly be theirs; Northerners realized that they must mobilize and train for an all-out and probably protracted war.

In the West, by early 1862 the Confederates had established a line of defense extending from the Mississippi, through Bowling Green, Kentucky, to Cumberland Gap, Virginia. At the center of this line, in Tennessee, protecting access to the Tennessee and Cumberland rivers, they erected Fort Henry and Fort Donelson, 12 miles apart. Mounting the first major Union offensive in the West, General Henry W. Halleck ordered General Ulysses S. Grant, at the head of a land and river expedition, to take the Rebel forts. Fort Henry fell under pounding from the Federal fleet on February 6. Ten days later the commander of Fort Donelson capitulated; asking for surrender terms, he learned from Grant that there were 'no terms but unconditional surrender.' With the two rivers now open to Union gunboats, and with easy access to the Southern heartland, the Union rejoiced in its new hero, 'Unconditional Surrender' Grant.

Grant moved southward with 43,000 men toward the rail center at Corinth, Mississippi. Attempting to prevent Grant's link-up with a 10,000-man force under Don Carlos Buell, Confederate General Albert Sidney Johnston brought his 40,000 troops to Shiloh, some 20 miles from his base at Corinth. P. G. T. Beauregard, Johnston's field commander, attacked on April 6, catching the Union by surprise and sending many of the Federal troops running. A division near the center held, however, giving the Federals a chance to rally. That afternoon Johnston was mortally wounded, and by evening Buell had arrived. On the next day Grant and Buell forced the Confederates to retreat to Corinth. At 'Bloody Shiloh' the Union suffered 13,000 casualties; the Confederates 10,000.

Johnston was succeeded by Braxton Bragg, and while Bragg and Grant maneuvered against each other, New Orleans fell (April 24) to the Union fleet under David G. Farragut, as did Baton Rouge and Natchez. The Confederates abandoned Corinth at the end of May.

In the East, General George B. McClellan was given command of the Union armies and spent the winter training the raw recruits streaming into the capital. Cautious to a degree that regularly infuriated Lincoln, McClellan refused to take an overland approach to Richmond but won Lincoln's approval for an approach from the southeastern end of the York-James peninsula. McDowell's corps of 37,000 would remain near Fredericksburg to ensure Washington's safety. McClellan's 105,000 men were moved to the tip of the peninsula by early April 1862. Under General Joseph E. Johnston, the Confederates established a thin grey line across the peninsula at historic Yorktown and withdrew their main 60,000-man force toward Richmond.

After a month-long siege of Yorktown – considered unnecessary by many – McClellan moved on Richmond, reaching Seven Pines some nine miles away. Here, and at nearby Fair Oaks, the Confederates halted the Union advance. Johnston, however, was severely wounded and was replaced as commander by General Robert E. Lee. Meanwhile, Stonewall Jackson's brilliant maneuvering of his small force in the

Shenandoah Valley effectively kept Washington from reinforcing McClellan, while constantly threatening the Union capital.

On June 25 Jackson joined with Lee in attacking McClellan's exposed right in order to foil the Union's second major attempt on Richmond. Lee made his decison to attack on the basis of field intelligence from his flamboyant cavalry commander J. E. B. Stuart, who had been raiding all around McClellan's force. Lee was also aware of his opponent's excessive caution. In the ensuing Seven Days' Campaign the Confederates first failed at Mechanicsville, but at Gaines' Mill, Lee forced McClellan to withdraw to his supply base on the James River, 20 miles distant from Richmond. Here McClellan was safe under the protective guns of Union gunboats, but his campaign had failed, and his troops would be evacuated from the peninsula in August.

Almost immediately a newly-formed 45,000-man Union Army of Virginia, under General John Pope, took the field in northern Virginia, with Richmond again as its goal. Lee advanced to central Virginia to keep Pope from cutting communication and supply lines between the Southern capital and the Shenandoah Valley. Splitting his force, he sent Stonewall Jackson's 23,000 men on a sweeping march north to Pope's rear, where they took the Union supply base at Manassas. On August 29 Pope found Jackson dug in near the old Bull Run battleground. Pope attacked but, too late, discovered that Lee had reunited his force with Jackson's. A Rebel counterattack then drove Pope from the field of this Second Battle of Bull Run. After a last encounter with Lee at Chantilly on September 1 Pope withdrew to Washington, where he asked to be relieved of his command.

With Virginia free of Northern soldiers, General Lee crossed the Potomac and took Frederick, Maryland. McClellan, commanding the Army of the Potomac, moved to meet him. Lee split his Army of Northern Virginia, sending Jackson south to take the Union garrison at Harpers Ferry while he marched to Hagerstown. By accident, a copy of Lee's plan came into McClellan's hands, and he hurried to split Lee and Jackson and cut their access to the Shenandoah. On September 17, 1862, the armies met at Antietam Creek, near Sharpsburg, Maryland, on what would be the bloodiest day of the war. The outnumbered Southerners, with their backs to the Potomac but facing uncoordinated attacks from McClellan, were able to hold their positions until the night of the 18th, when they withdrew across the river. But they had taken 13,000 casualties (to the Union's 12,500), and their offensive in Maryland had been turned aside.

McClellan's failure to pursue Lee actively cost him his command. Lincoln replaced him with the well-meaning but limited Ambrose E. Burnside. With Richmond again the target, Burnside crossed the Rappahannock at Fredericksburg, Virginia, on December 11-12, and on the 13th mounted repeated assaults on Lee's army, well-entrenched on the heights west and south of town. Burnside achieved nothing and lost 12,600 men; Lee lost 5300.

In the West, in the summer of 1862, Braxton Bragg and his Army of Tennessee moved to unite Kentucky with the Confederacy. Union General Don Carlos Buell, who had been moving toward Chattanooga, at once turned his forces toward Louisville. Advance units of the two armies met at Perryville on October 8, and a skirmish turned into an indecisive battle that cost Bragg 3400 and Buell 4200. But Bragg was nevertheless forced to withdraw from Kentucky to a position on Stone's River near Murfreesboro, Tennessee. Here, on the last day of 1862, Bragg met the Union Army of the Cumberland under William S. Rosecrans. (General Rosecrans had received his command for having successfully repulsed a two-day Confederate assault on Corinth by Generals Earl Van Dorn and Sterling Price early in October.) Bragg first crushed Rosecrans' right but was then thrown back after attacking George H. Thomas at the Union center. Bragg lost 11,300, Rosecrans 13,200, almost one-third of their forces. On January 3, 1863, the Confederate army moved southward to Tullahoma in central Tennessee. So far, the war had gone mostly in favor of the South, but the new year now beginning, 1863, would tell a different story.

Right: A contemporary drawing of a train carrying troops of General Joseph E. Johnston's Confederate Army of Shenandoah to Manassas Junction, where they were being massed to fight in the Battle of Bull Run.

Below: Union Generals Irvin McDowell and George B. McClellan and their staffs being escorted by a unit of cavalry across the stream known as Bull Run.

Left: A sketch by artist A. R. Waud of troops from Rhode Island and New York brigades at Bull Run on July 18. Two weeks later, an engraving of the scene was printed in the *New York Illustrated News*.

Below left: Union soldiers attempt to reverse the Confederate assault and prevent a complete rout.

Below: General Thomas J. Jackson, whose Confederate troops stood like a stone wall on Henry House Hill on July 21. They held fast against all Union charges until the Federals were driven back in defeat.

Opposite: A commemorative painting (1889) celebrates the First Battle of Bull Run.

Top left: Union Colonel Michael Corcoran leads his Irish troops in an attack.

Top right: A charge by Union Zouaves against Rebel Black Horse Cavalry.

Left: Union Colonel Ambrose E. Burnside's brigade of Rhode Island volunteers led a turning movement around the Confederate flank. In the following month Burnside would be promoted to general, and within 15 months he would be asked by Lincoln to take over McClellan's command of the Army of the Potomac.

Above: Engraving of a last stand by McDowell's men at Manassas.

Right: The home of Wilmer McLean near Manassas Junction served as the headquarters of Confederate General P. G. T. Beauregard at Bull Run. To avoid danger, McLean relocated to Appomattox Court House, where four years later his new home would be the site of Lee's surrender to Grant.

Below: The Stone House near the Warrenton Turnpike was at the center of the fighting at Bull Run.

Left: Ruins of the Stone Bridge over Bull Run. The bridge was an anchor of the Confederate position at dawn on July 21, but by the end of the day it saw the panicky Union retreat.

Left below: The Manassas railroad junction in March 1862, destroyed by retreating Confederate forces in the path of the Union advance.

Below Andrew Hull Foote commanded the flotilla of Union gunboats that supported Grant's army in the taking of Fort Henry and Fort Donelson in February 1862.

Below right: General John Charles Frémont commanded the Western Department. His guard is shown charging through Springfield, Missouri, on October 24, 1861. A noted explorer, as well as the Republican presidential nominee in 1856, Frémont embarrassed Lincoln by a number of political and military mistakes and was relieved of command.

Opposite top left: General Ulysses S. Grant's ability to rally his troops was displayed at Fort Donelson when he urged his frightened soldiers to take the Confederate fortifications.

Opposite top right: On September 17, 1862, Union General George W. Morgan blew up the arsenal he had established at the Cumberland Gap rather than face a Confederate siege. He then marched 200 miles through wilderness to the Ohio River. A year later, the Gap was returned to Union possession by General Burnside.

Opposite bottom: An engraving of the capture of Fort Donelson. Grant's taking of forts Henry and Donelson, with more than 14,000 prisoners, was the first major Union victory. It delighted the North and brought the general to Lincoln's attention.

Below: General William Tecumseh Sherman organized the division of Union volunteers that he commanded at the Battle of Shiloh. He was seriously wounded in the fighting. General Grant said of him, 'to his individual efforts I am indebted for the success of that battle.'

Right: At the Battle of Shiloh, or Pittsburg Landing, General Ulysses S. Grant was surprised by Johnston's attack in the early morning of April 6, 1862. After the battle, to demands that Grant be dismissed, Lincoln responded, 'I can't spare this man, he fights.'

Above: Union reinforcements arrive at the Hornet's Nest, a center of Federal resistance at Shiloh. The position, commanded by Benjamin Prentiss, held against 12 Southern assaults, giving Grant time to form a defensive line.

Right: Union troops rally under the bluffs of the Tennessee River where they had been driven by the first attack. Artillery at Pittsburg Landing and cannon fire from Union gunboats *Lexington* and *Tyler* support their defensive line.

Opposite: Engraving from a painting by Alonzo Chappal: the recapture of Union artillery by General L. H. Rosseau.

Right: General Don Carlos Buell marched his troops through swamps from Savannah to Pittsburg Landing. Their arrival as Grant's troops were being driven back checked the Rebel assault and aided Grant in taking the offensive on April 7.

Far right: General Lewis Wallace brought his 5000 men from Crump's Landing, five miles below Pittsburg Landing, to join Buell's fresh troops on the night of April 6.

Below: On the second day of fighting General Grant leads his army forward in the last Union charge at Shiloh. The largest battle ever waged on the American continent, it cost the North 13,000 casualties, the South 10,000.

Below right: Confederate General Braxton Bragg commanded a corps at Shiloh. He succeeded Beauregard in June as commander of the Army of Tennessee.

Below: In March 1862, Union troops under General John Pope captured New Madrid, Missouri, putting them into position to attack the Confederate garrison on nearby Island No.10 in the Mississippi River. It fell without a fight on April 7, after Federal gunboats reduced its shore batteries.

Below right: Adm. David G. Farragut, photographed in New Orleans in 1863, led a Union fleet up the Mississippi River to New Orleans, seizing the undefended city on April 25, 1862. He lost only one ship while running the confederate river defenses.

Right: The Union occupied the city of Baton Rouge in May 1862, but in August a Confederate force under John C. Breckinridge, assisted by the ironclad ram *Arkansas*, attempted to recapture it. After a six-hour battle the Rebels were repulsed, and the gunboat was destroyed.

Opposite top: The burning of the Louisiana state capitol at Baton Rouge shortly after Union troops occupied the city.

Opposite bottom: Confederate fire ships bear down on the Union fleet in an attempt to break the blockade at the mouth of the Mississippi on October 12, 1861.

Left: Union guns and munitions on a wharf at Yorktown, Virginia, in May 1862. The Confederates evacuated before the overwhelming force of McClellan's Army of the Potomac as it advanced slowly up the Peninsula toward Richmond.

Right: General George B. McClellan (hatless, with sash) and his staff in March 1862 when Lincoln gave him the Army of the Potomac and acquiesced to his plan for entering Virginia by way of the southeastern peninsula.

Above left: A battery of Union horse artillery moves up in the Battle of Fair Oaks. Here, Confederate General Joseph E. Johnston halted the Union advance in the Peninsular Campaign, but, severely wounded in the battle, he was replaced as commander of the Army of Northern Virginia by General Robert E. Lee.

Above: General George Stoneman and his staff at Fair Oaks. Stoneman was McClellan's chief of cavalry and was later governor of California.

Far left: Confederate General Thomas J. ('Stonewall') Jackson in a Mathew Brady portrait made two weeks before his death on May 10, 1863. Called by Lee the outstanding soldier of the war, Jackson conducted a brilliant campaign in the spring of 1862 to control the Shenandoah Valley. His small force of fast-moving infantry effectively prevented reinforcement of McClellan on the Peninsula, all the while threatening Washington with attack.

Left: A skirmish in the Shenandoah Valley on June 7 between units of Jackson's army and a company of Pennsylvania infantry.

Below: View of Front Royal, Virginia, where on May 23, 1862, Jackson routed a large Federal force. Two days later, at Winchester, Jackson and General Richard Ewell attacked General Nathaniel Banks, forcing him to withdraw across the Potomac to Federal territory.

Right: Field artist Alfred R. Waud captured this clash between Federals and Jackson's Confederates (behind the stone wall) on March 23, 1862. Such skirmishes persuaded Lincoln that McDowell should not participate in the Peninsular Campaign but stay behind to defend Washington.

Far right: General John C. Frémont, beaten by Jackson in the Shenandoah Valley, was put under General Pope's command but asked to be relieved in June rather than serve.

Right: Union General Nathaniel P. Banks, defeated by Stonewall Jackson at Front Royal and Winchester, would meet and be defeated by him again in August at Cedar Mountain, Virginia, at the start of Second Bull Run.

Right: In the Seven Days' Campaign, Union forces under General Fitz-John Porter beat back the Confederate attack at Mechanicsville on June 26, 1862, but on the next day Lee broke the Federal lines at Gaines' Mill.

Below: The Battle of Williamsburg on May 5, 1862, engaged Confederate troops evacuating Yorktown and the Federals advancing up the peninsula.

Left: Lee's colorful cavalry chief, General J. E. B. Stuart, circled McClellan's entire Union army on the Peninsula, raiding and reconnoitering for three days, June 12-14, providing Lee with the intelligence he needed to launch his offensive.

Above left: A. R. Waud's sketch of Confederates advancing to capture disabled guns at Gaines' Mill. In an all-day fight the Rebels broke the Federal lines. McClellan retired to his supply base on the James River.

Above: The headquarters of Robert E. Lee during the Battle of Gaines' Mill. Although Lee failed to cripple the Army of the Potomac, his offensive thwarted for a second time the Union attempt on Richmond.

Left: A view of Mechanicsville, where Lee launched an offensive to drive the Union from Virginia. It is only nine miles from Richmond.

Despite the Northern bias displayed in the painting on this page and the Currier & Ives print on the facing page, the Second Battle of Bull Run was not a success for the Union. The campaign, also known as Second Manassas, began in mid-July when General John Pope began massing a large force in northern Virginia. In August, Lee moved northward to meet him before the additional reinforcements could arrive from McClellan's Army of the Potomac. Lee's movements were

known to Pope, but he was unaware that Jackson, with half the Southern force, had maneuvered to encircle him near the old Bull Run battlefield. When additional Southern troops under Longstreet arrived, the difference between the sizes of the two opposing forces was reduced. Pope's soldiers found themselves no match for the well prepared Confederates. The final engagement of the campaign occurred at Chantilly, Virginia, on September 1, 1862. Pope withdrew to

Washington, and command of his Union Army of Virginia was given to McClellan. Lee's state of Virginia was now free of Federal troops, and he then moved his Army of Northern Virginia across the Potomac River into Maryland, taking Frederick and threatening the national capital.

Above: Drawing by Edwin Forbes of Pope's troops withdrawing from the battle with Jackson's men near Groveton on August 28. On the next day Pope moved against the Southern force at Manassas, thinking they would retreat, but he found himself outmatched by Jackson and Longstreet at the Second battle of Bull Run.

Right: Two photographers have lunch by the Bull Run before the battle.

Right: Drawing by Edwin Forbes of the old defenses at the Bull Run battlefield in April 1862.

Left: Federal troops under Colonel Chapman assault a Confederate force defending a railroad embankment during the peak of the fighting at Second Bull Run.

Above: Major General "Fighting Joe" Hooker, commander of the Union 1st Corps, mounted a strong attack on the Confederate left that resulted in heavy casualties on both sides.

Left: Union soldiers advance against outnumbered Confederates on September 17, 1862, at the Battle of Antietam. General Lee's men held their ground on this bloodiest day of the war, but drew back across the Potomac to Virginia on the 18th.

Above: After several unsuccessful attempts, Union troops under General Ambrose E. Burnside advance across the bridge (that now bears his name) at Antietam Creek. They were halted by the arrival of A. P. Hill. It has been suggested that Burnside could simply have forded the stream rather than force the bridge.

Right: A detail of the battlefield at Antietam, Union horse artillery on the left, infantry on the right. The photograph was made by Alexander Gardner, who had been hired by Mathew Brady in the late 1850s to manage his photo gallery. Gardner later claimed credit for the idea of compiling a photo history of the Civil War, but credit is now generally given to Brady.

Below: Colonel Burnside and his staff of the First Rhode Island Volunteers, the corps he commanded at the First Battle of Bull Run.

Right: Union soldiers at a signal station on Elk Mountain, Maryland, in October 1862, overlooking the now-quiet Antietam battleground.

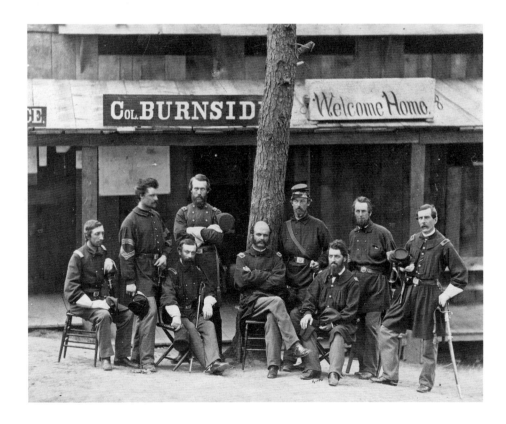

Above: President Lincoln conferring with McClellan and his generals at Harpers Ferry after the Battle of Antietam. After months of supporting McClellan, Lincoln removed him as commander of the Army of the Potomac and gave the command to Burnside in early November 1862.

Right: Burnside (Sharpsburg) Bridge over Antietam Creek.

Below: A painting of the Battle of Fredericksburg by Frederick Cavada. The Northern troops are attempting to storm the large Southern force well entrenched on Marye's Heights behind Fredericksburg, Virginia. It was described by one Union soldier as 'a great slaughter pen.'

Right: As Union engineers trying to lay a pontoon bridge come under fire, troops embark across the Rappahannock at Fredericksburg.

Left: General Ambrose E. Burnside commanded a Union army numbering about 106,000; Lee's Southerners totaled about 72,000.

Below: Union troops move across one bridge as engineers work to lay another across the Rappahannock on December 11, 1862.

Right: Wounded Confederate soldiers on Marye's Heights. The casualties on December 13 totaled 12,600 for the Union, 5300 for the South.

Below: A view of Fredericksburg from the river, showing Confederate troops at the foot of the wrecked bridge.

Below right: A Union ambulance corps removing the dead from the battlefield at Fredericksburg. Lee refrained from attacking Burnside's men as they withdrew.

Left: The Confederate defenders' trench at the foot of Marye's Heights, four months after the fighting.

Left below: Dead are interred in a hospital graveyard in Fredericksburg. The battle gained Burnside nothing, and he was replaced in January 1863.

Right: The Confederate defeat in the battle at Mill Springs, Kentucky, opened a gap in the Southern defense line in the Kentucky-Tennessee area. The Rebel commander General Felix Zollicoffer was killed.

Opposite top left: The Union left at the Battle of Perryville, Kentucky. The largest of a number of battles in the state, it pitted Union troops under Don Carlos Buell against the Army of Tennessee under Braxton Bragg on October 8-9, 1862. General Bragg was forced to retreat southeast into Tennessee, where he would meet Union General Rosecrans at Murfreesboro at the end of the year.

Opposite top right: Union artillery and infantry face a Confederate attack on their position on Stone's River near Murfreesboro, Tennessee, on December 31, 1862. Although the Confederate force under Braxton Bragg generally controlled the three-day fighting, Bragg withdrew when he found that the enemy force had been resupplied.

Below: At Corinth, Mississippi, on October 4, 1862, Union defenders under William S. Rosecrans, halt a Rebel offensive aimed at taking the railroad center.

Opposite bottom: Union encampment at Corinth, Mississippi, in May 1862. An important strategic point, Corinth was the scene of battle in May and again in early October 1862.

The Armies

When the Civil War began, the U.S. Army totaled only about 16,000 men, with most of them posted on the western frontier; and the state militias had no training for battle. When the call went out for volunteers, young men in both the North and South crowded the recruiting stations to enlist in the great adventure. Regiments were raised by the states. In the North volunteers generally signed on for three years, in the South for 12 months. As enlistment periods expired and enthusiasm for fighting waned, conscription laws were enacted. In the South, on April 16, 1862, the Confederate Congress passed a draft law making all men 18 to 35 (later 17 to 50) liable for the duration. In the North conscription for 20- to 45-year-olds for a period of three years was enacted a year later, on March 3, 1863, but there were exemptions for those who could hire a substitute. After Lincoln's Emancipation Proclamation in January 1863, Union companies of black soldiers were raised. (In the South blacks were armed in desperation in 1865). Continuous recruiting and veteran reenlistments, however, meant that conscripts – who were often of doubtful quality as soldiers – never formed an important part of either army. A total of about 1,500,000 men served in the North; 1,000,000 in the South. At the end of the war 800,000 Union soldiers faced 200,000 Confederates.

Typically, locally-raised companies with elected officers joined similar units at a state training camp. After basic training, ten volunteer companies were joined as a regiment; regimental commanders would often be amateurs, since the regular army officers usually remained with their regular army units. Training consisted mainly of drill, moving from marching formations to combat formations and back again. The amount of target practice was limited, on the assumption (unfounded, as it turned out) that most men were competent with a musket.

Uniforms covered a broad spectrum, from the elaborate dress uniform of the Southern cavalry officer to the ornate, brightly colored French-Algerian style of the Zouaves, to the nondescript, often scavenged clothing worn by many Southern infantrymen. Customarily, the Union soldier's uniform was dark blue; the Rebel's was officially gray but was often a butternut yellow-brown when the cloth had been dyed in a solution of nutshells. The Union soldier usually carried a knapsack for his spare clothing, a shoulder bag for his rations, and an overcoat and a blanket; the Confederate often carried only the last.

Cavalrymen were armed with a saber, a light-weight carbine, and a pistol. Regular infantrymen carried a 'rifle musket,' essentially an old-fashioned muzzle-loader with a rifled barrel, often called a 'Springfield' for its place of manufacture in Massachusetts. In addition, heavy-barreled target rifles such as the Sharps were used for sniping, and there were some repeating rifles, such as the Henry , which was able to fire 15 shots without reloading. These rifled weapons had far greater accuracy and range than their smoothbore ancestors, and, because tactics well into the war remained pretty much as they had been before the advent of the new weapons, the result was that massed soldiers attempting to maneuver to within 100 yards of each other could be met by killing fire 1000 yards from their goal. The use of machine guns was limited. The most effective was the Billinghurst-Requa battery gun, consisting of 25 rifle barrels mounted side by side on a light carriage. Also, about 60 single-barrel Ager guns, loaded from a cranked hopper, were purchased by the Union army, as were a dozen Gatling guns, which used six barrels rotating around a central spindle. These last were not employed until the siege of Petersburg in 1864, but they continued in use by the U.S. Army until World War I.

Rifled-bore artillery could reach a smooth-bore battery while remaining beyond range of counterfire. However, most of the 50 or so types of artillery pieces used in the war were smooth-bores, such as the omnipresent breech-loading 12-pounder.

The huge increase in firepower in the Civil War as compared with previous wars resulted in an enormous increase in the number of casualties, particularly since capable leaders able to adapt strategies to the new weapons were slow to emerge. Some 350,000 Union soldiers and 400,000 Confederates died (although perhaps two-thirds of them died from infection and disease). In a number of campaigns, more than half the troops engaged fell in battle.

Bad hygiene, bad water, and bad food took a huge toll. Medical remedies were nonexistent or ineffective. Ambulance service in the field was haphazard, and the wounded might remain unattended for hours or days. At its best – and both sides tried their best – the system would tend to a soldier's wounds at a regimental aid station, take him to a divisional hospital well behind the lines for further treatment or major surgery, then move him to a base hospital in the rear, perhaps by hospital train. But given the limited supply of physicians and surgeons available for service, the quality of medical care was often poor, and even the best doctors of the time possessed only the most meager knowledge of the causes of wound infection or disease. Some doctors had made the connection between sanitation and disease, but the idea of sterilizing instruments or dressings had not even occurred. The poor recovery rate caused general distrust of the medical department among the men.

Between campaigns ordinary soldiers would drill (and drill), perform sentry duty, tend their clothing and equipment, and see to their meals, which in the South often meant foraging and doing their own cooking. They lived mostly in tents but might erect various wooden shelters when they went into winter quarters, when there was otherwise little else to do.

Authorized daily rations for the Federal soldier included about a pound each of meat and bread or flour, and a quarter pound each of potatoes and peas or beans. (His Confederate counterpart was allotted about half that amount of meat.) Locally-purchased fruits and vegetables were expected to round out the diet. Often, when the soldier was at the end of a long and weakened supply line, he was issued less than authorized, and even that might be tainted or unpalatable. Supply scandals were common. In both armies private operators, or 'sutlers,'

were permitted to accompany the regiment in wagons and provide, at regulated prices, whatever food, tobacco, and condiments they could carry. In the North the Quartermaster corps supplied boots, uniforms, tents, and blankets to all the men. In the South each state had responsibility for its own regiments, and one state's surplus might be stored rather than distributed to needy soldiers from another state.

Unlike European wars, where the territory the armies fought on was well mapped, the Civil War was fought on land that had not been completely surveyed and where roads and bridges were insufficient to move large forces, equipment, and supplies. The military engineers had to create both maps and surface roads, as well as span rivers, lay track, operate ferries, string telegraph lines, prepare trenches, and erect fortifications. The Union army had a strong corps of officers with engineering training who could train field engineers. The Confederate army had no such corps, often employing civil engineers and commandeered infantrymen as needed.

Among the most dreadful institutions of the war were the prisons for captured enemy troops. During the war each side took some 200,000 prisoners of war. Attempts were made to exchange prisoners, but most captured soldiers went to prisons, and 56,000 died there. The worst prisons were no more than walled compounds, with no provisions for shelter, water, or sanitation. None would be considered habitable by modern conventions. Among the more infamous were Elmira prison camp in New York, Johnson Island in Lake Erie, some converted warehouses in Richmond, and, doubtless worst of all, the stockade at Andersonville, Georgia. Conditions at Andersonville were so horrendous that at the end of the war its superintendent was convicted of murder by a military court and hanged. The graves of its 13,000 dead enlisted men are today a national historic site.

Left: A Currier & Ives print of a Union officer departing for the war. At the start of the war most of the general officers were academy-trained professional soldiers. At the company and regimental levels, however, they often were state appointees or men elected by the soldiers themselves.

Opposite: Men of the 96th Pennsylvania Infantry Regiment during drill at Camp Northumberland, Pennsylvania, in 1861. Such exercises were essential in teaching the men to move quickly from marching formation to battle formation under field conditions.

Left: A recruiting poster for the Federal navy issued in 1863. The Union navy had the responsibility for blockading 3000 miles of Confederate coastline and supporting invasions mounted on inland and coastal waters.

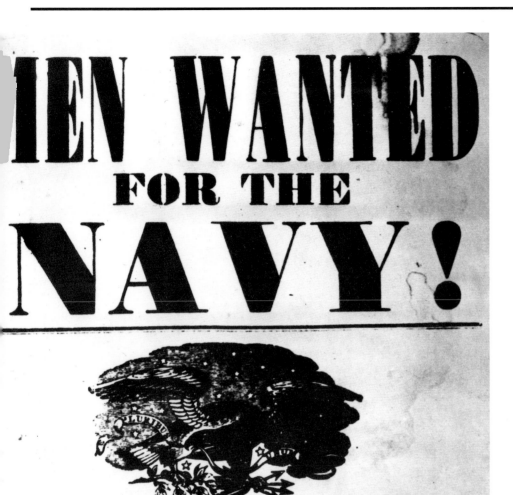

Right below: A Louisiana 'Pelican.' Confederate soldiers increasingly had to make do with whatever uniforms and equipment were available as the war drew on.

Opposite left: A private of the 11th New York Infantry, the 'Fire Zouaves.' It is the Unit of Elmer E. Ellsworth, the first Union commissioned officer to die in the Civil War.

Opposite top right: The officer's mess table and utensils used in the war by then major Rutherford B. Hayes.

Opposite bottom right: A Confederate shoe made from leather and wood. It represents the difficulties the South faced in keeping its troops supplied.

Right: An out-of-uniform private of the 4th Michigan Infantry. Union troops were generally better-dressed, better-armed, and better-supplied than their Confederate counterparts.

Opposite: Company F of the 14th Pennsylvania Infantry in August 1864. State militia and volunteer units often adopted such nonstandard exotic uniforms, which were very popular with the public in both the North and South.

Right: A belt model and Dragoon model (disassembled) of Wesson & Leavitt patented revolvers manufactured by the Massachusetts Arms Company. Many of these revolvers, made in the early 1850s, were used in the Civil War.

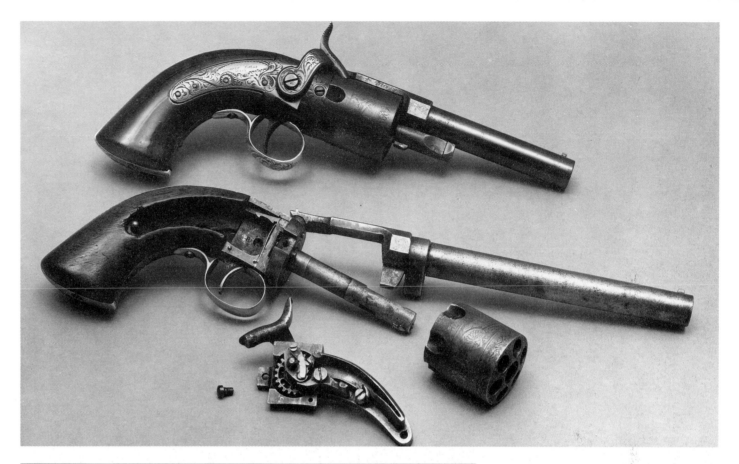

Left: Owing to the immediate need at the start of the war, a few thousand Model 1842 .69 caliber percussion muskets were issued to Union troops from storage. These were fitted with an updated priming system.

Right: Patent drawing of the Spencer carbine, the weapon of choice of most Union cavalry regiments. It was a shortened version of the Spencer infantry model, which is considered the first successful repeating rifle.

Right below: Savage .36 Navy model, *c*.1865, fitted with a shoulder stock and a long-range sight. Many soldiers preferred .36 caliber ('Navy') revolvers to the heavier .44 caliber ('Army') weapons.

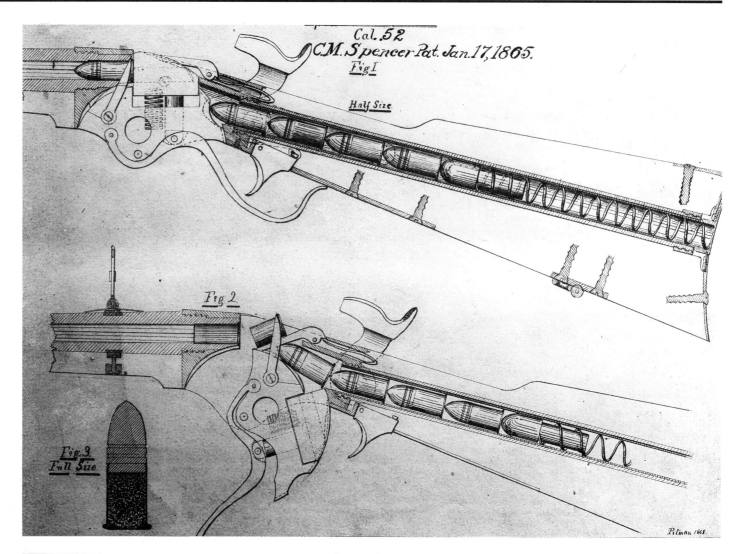

CARBINES

r last catalogue was issued, the gun market has undergone quite a change, by reason of the United States Government selling off guns to the highest bidder that had been held at high-limit prices. We purchased the largest lot, and at once interested some of the large department stores, to whom we sold many thousands a quarter of our former prices. realizing a fair profit for a quick turn of the money invested. We reserved a number of the choicest and rarest of these car- rich will now be found on this and following pages. The low prices at which many of these carbines were sold by the department stores throughout the country many to start a collection. To such this catalogue will be valuable, enabling them to add further specimens.

German Mauser 43-calibre Breech-loading Centre-fire Rifled Carbine. Used by German Cavalry. Guns are in good serviceable order. Bolt action. Price, $6.80 each.

German Mauser 43-calibre Repeating Rifled Carbine, Model 1884, in fine order; like new guns. Bolt action. Price, $9.80 each.

Peabody Breech-loading Rifled Carbines. 50-calibre. Rim fire. In serviceable order. Lever action. Made by famous Providence Tool Co., which furnished 600,000 Pea- body guns to the Sultan of Turkey. Price, per gun, $1.75. Ball or blank cartridges, $1.50 per 100.

Gallagher Breech-loading Rifled Carbines, 50 calibre. Rim fire. Shooting same car- tridges as the Spencer and Peabody rifles. New guns. Rare relics, as only a few were made to take metallic cartridges. Lever action with patch box in stock. Price, $6.50 each.

Ballard Breech-loading Rifled Carbine. 50 calibre. Rim fire. In fair, serviceable order. Lever action. Positive extractor. Relics. Price, $8.75 each.

Merrill Breech-loading Rifled Car- bine. For use with percussion cap. Used in Civil War, 1861-65. In service- able order. Calibre 54. Price, $6.95 each.

Sharp & Hankins Breech- loading Rifled 50-calibre Rim fire Rifled Carbine. Shoots the rim fire cartridge. Lever slides the barrel forward, leaving the empty cartridge shell impinged on stationary extractor in the breech. Novel and rare mechanism. These guns are now very scarce. Price. $10.00 each. In serviceable order.

urnside Breech-loading Rifled Carbines. Calibre 54. Shooting etallic cartridge with the percussion cap. We can furnish these s at $1.50 per 100. Guns are in good serviceable order. Price, h, with 30 cartridges. Packed 10 in case.

Joslyn Breech-loading Cap and Ball Rifled Carbine. Calibre 54. Used in latter part of the Civil War. Good serviceable second-hand order. Price, $3.25 each.

rd Breech-loading Rifled Carbine. Calibre 50. Light, neat, e. Metallic cartridge fired with percussion cap. We have large of these cartridges. Cost the Government $18.00 each. Invented aynard, the originator of the patent primer bearing his name. Gun d by the lever. Chiefly valuable as relic of Civil War period. a 30 cartridges, price $5.90 each.

100 Sharp's Heavy Octagon-barrel Breech-load- ing Cap and Ball Rifled Carbines. Used by Civil War sharpshooters. In good serviceable order. Calibres are various, from 40 to 50. Have the lever action. Weight about 10 pounds. Valuable relics. Finest kind of shoot- ing has been done with these guns. We have no cartridges. With bullet mold from the Ideal Co., New Haven, sportsmen could, with little expense, make their own cartridges. Price, $6.80 each.

1,000 Seven-shot Spencer Repeating Rifle Carbines. 50 calibre Rim fire. Made under the supervision of inventor C. M. Spencer. Magazine is in the butt stock and holds seven cartridges, while one can be inserted in the magazine. An effective rifle for hunting or defense. Shot cartridges can be used in this gun as made by all the cartridge companies. Barrel is 22 inches long. Weight about 7 pounds. used as a single-loader, holding the magazine in reserve. Edward Stabler was the inventor, a peace-loving Quaker, who took to hunting to recover lost health. His home was in Maryland. Is worked by a lever, same as in the Winchester or Marlin— simplest, safest and best mechanism in repeating gun. Fine walnut stock. Has a record of 7 shots in 20 seconds. These guns are new; are still in the original factory cases; steel barrels, case hardened steel mechanism. Price for one of these new

3.50 ave a few hundred of these Spencer Repeating Carbines which have been in use and which are in serviceable order, not refinished, and the price for single gun We have a few hundred Spencer Repeating Carbines which have been worn out in service; are not in shooting order; are valuable only to gunsmiths for other guns; are incomplete in parts, and which we offer as War Relics only. Price, $1.80 for single gun; $15.00 for case of 10 guns. We can supply many Spencer Carbines and Rifles, including new walnut stocks. Write us what part you require and we will quote price.

700,000 Spencer Copper Shell, Rim fire, 50 calibre Ball Cartridges; made to use in Spencer guns. We have sold hun- dreds of thousands of these cartridges and have had second and third orders. We have tested many of these cartridges and never yet found one that missed fire. Nevertheless we offer them as they are—as they were made up many years ago. Price, $1.50 per 100; $13.75 per 1,000. 50,000 Spencer Rim fire Blank Cartridges. 50 calibre, for saluting purposes. Price, $1.50 per 100: $13.75 per 1,000. Spencer Rim fire, 50 calibre Cartridges, loaded with bird shot which we obtain from the American Cartridge Company at price of 60 cents for box of 25 cartridges. We only offer to supply Bird Shot

.36 .50

ncer Copper Cartridge. oaded with Lead Ball.

Spencer Copper Cartridge. Filled with Bird Shot.

Spencer Blank Cartridge, Copper Shell.

s when ordered with our Spencer guns. 20 Spencer Carbines, like new, with bright instead of blue barrels. Price, $3.35 each.

Colonel who represented the Southern Confederacy in Europe during the Civil War, purchasing arms and war material to be shipped to the South by blockade teamers, while in our store related an incident that may interest our readers: That after the Civil War was over he was in France trying to sell to the French ent some of the large quantities of arms left over from the war and had met with poor success getting through the red tape which surrounded the French War when meeting Mr. Slidell, he whose forcible removal from a British ship while on his way to Europe to represent the Southern Confederacy came near bringing between the United States and Great Britain, Slidell suggested that the Colonel go and see the Emperor (Napoleon III). So the Colonel wrote to the Em- received an invitation to call at the palace at Versailles. On showing the Emperor the Spencer Repeating Carbine and working through the mechanism 7 dummy a few seconds, the Emperor exclaimed, "Why, no army could carry sufficient cartridges to supply such quick-firing guns." The Colonel had his answer read ed: "Emperor, you have seen the gentle, lingering summer shower. also the sudden, destructive hail storm, which lasts but a short time but does great dam- e ordinary breech-loading gun is like the summer rain, the Spencer Repeater like the destructive hail storm." The Colonel was sent to the Minister of War der to relieve the Emperor gave Colonel —— a small order, as he seemed provoked that he had not first been consulted. We believe this was the same War who prior to the Franco-Prussian War assured Emperor Napoleon that the French army was all equipped ready for war even down to the soldier's shoe strings had the French army been armed with Spencer Repeating Rifles the map of Europe would now show Alsace and Lorraine as part of the French Empire.

Left: Page from the catalog of a commerical gun dealer, featuring some of the rifles used during the Civil War.

Top: Some of the uniforms of the Army of the Confederacy.

Above: A Colt .36 Navy model of 1851, with blued finish. Colt revolvers were the most common pistols used in the war. The most popular were the 1851 Navy, 1861 Navy, and 1860 Army.

Opposite: A private of the 22nd New York militia guards a 12-pounder Napoleon smooth-bore at Harpers Ferry. The 12-pounder was the principal field gun of both Union and Confederacy.

Left: Men of Company C, 41st New York Infantry at Manassas in July 1862. They are perched on breastworks made from earth and timbers and rough baskets filled with rocks and dirt.

Below left: The .58 caliber Ager machine gun, called the 'Coffee Mill' for its cranked feed hopper.

Below: A gun designed for short-range intensive fire, the Billinghurst-Requa Battery Gun had 25 rifle barrels mounted side by side.

Below: Officers of the 55th New York Infantry examine a Rebel 24-pounder used at Fort Gaines in defense of Mobile Bay.

Right: An imported British Armstrong 150-pounder rifled gun used in the defense of Fort Fisher in Wilmington, North Carolina.

Below right: Defending Washington is this 15-inch Rodman gun, among the last giants of the smooth-bore era.

Right: A battery of 12-pounders in the Union artillery depot at City Point, Virginia.

Right below: Union 100-lb Parrott guns used in the siege of Yorktown in May 1862. These are rifled guns of cast iron reinforced at the breech end with a wrought-iron tube.

Left: The Union 'Dictator,' a 13-inch siege mortar used in the bombardment of Richmond. It was usually mounted on a railroad flatcar.

Opposite top left: A Union 32-pounder smooth-bore cannon used at Petersburg. It was mounted on a heavy railroad flatcar and was protected by a wood and iron shield.

Opposite top right: The experimental 900-pound Wiard gun. The elaborate casting was designed to lighten the gun without sacrificing strength. It was not a success.

Left: An armored railroad car with artillery, built to protect repair crews reconstructing burned bridges on the Philadelphia, Wilmington & Baltimore and B & O railroads.

Below: Women civilian volunteers were prepared to defend the Union. As the war progressed, the army employed more and more women as nursing staff in base hospitals.

Left: Soldiers of the Quartermaster Corps at the Union ordnance depot at City Point, Virginia. The two railroad engines in the background were both built in 1862 as part of the Union mobilization effort.

Opposite: Supplies for McClellan's army in the Peninsular Campaign are brought to a landing on the James River. Waiting wagon trains run by the Quartermaster Corps shuttle the supplies to the field.

Left: Men of the Military Telegraph Corps operating a field telegraph station with the Army of the Potomac in 1864. The corps of about 150 men, mainly civilians, was separate from the Signal Corps.

Below left: A U.S. Military Telegraph Corps wagon at Army of the Potomac headquarters near Petersburg in June 1864.

Below: Stringing telegraph line for the Army of the Potomac in April 1864. The U.S. Military Telegraph Corps served the Army of the Potomac through the Peninsular Campaign and at Fredericksburg and Chancellorsville.

Opposite: The Federal Balloon Corps, organized in 1862, provided aerial platforms for observing and artillery spotting. Here a balloon is filled with gas from hydrogen generators. Confederate attempts to form balloon units met with failure.

A Confederate Bull Battery Previous to the Battle of Bull Run

Opposite top: A Confederate officer sketched this 'bull battery' of oxen drawing heavy artillery before the Battle of Bull Run.

Opposite bottom: Union field engineers finish a bridge over the Chickahominy on June 18, 1862, before the start of the Seven Days' Campaign. The soil and straw covering protects the bridge from the pounding of horses and wagons.

Left: Union army engineers built the Chain Bridge across the Potomac at Georgetown. Bridge building was both a wartime and peacetime responsibility of the Corps of Engineers.

Above: A Union supply train crosses the Rappahannock below Fredericksburg on a pontoon bridge.

Opposite: Laborers erect a defensive stockade at Alexandria, Virginia.

Above left: Company kitchen of the 6th New York Artillery at Brandy Station, Virginia, in April 1864.

Left: A chimney built during winter quarters at Brandy Station in 1863-64.

Above: The 50th New York Engineers built an elaborate camp, including this beautiful wooden church, near Petersburg, Virginia.

Left: Families visit the camp of the 31st Pennsylvania Infantry near Washington, D.C., in 1862.

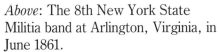

Above: The 8th New York State Militia band at Arlington, Virginia, in June 1861.

Above right: A group of officers of the Army of the Potomac take their ease at Fairfax Court House in June 1863. The kneeling officer is Count Ferdinand von Zeppelin, a German military observer who later achieved fame as a builder of rigid airships.

Right: Union officers enjoy cards and drink in one of their number's personal quarters.

Above: Men of the 18th Pennsylvania Cavalry at their winter quarters in February 1864. The canvas-covered roofs and barrel-topped chimneys were common features.

Left: Bombproof quarters of heavy logs and earth at a Union camp near Petersburg.

Left: Winter quarters of Union troops at Fort Brady in Virginia, on the James River.

Right: Soldiers lounge outside a South Carolina home that has been taken over as a military barracks.

Opposite: Sunday morning service in the camp of the 69th New York Infantry Regiment, the 'Fighting Irish.'

Above: An Army picture gallery set up in a tent.

Top right: An officer of the 3rd Pennsylvania Cavalry napping in his field quarters at Westover Landing, Virginia, in August 1862.

Right below: Two officers of Gen. A. A. Humphrey's staff rest in the shade near their field quarters.

Left: An amputation being performed outside a hospital tent at Gettysburg in July 1863. Ordinarily, this would be one of some 20 tents set up as a divisional hospital. First aid would be administered at the regimental level.

Above: Soldiers recuperating at Carver Hospital in Washington, D.C., in September 1864. By this time Northern medical facilities could provide much better care than that available in the South.

Top right: An infantryman of General R. S. Ewell's II Corps of the Army of Northern Virginia, killed at the Battle of Gettysburg.

Right below: A wounded soldier at an abandoned camp.

Right: An exhibit of utensils and other remains from the notorious Andersonville prison camp in Georgia.

Below: Libby Prison (shown) and Castle Thunder, both converted warehouses in Richmond, Virginia, are ranked among the worst of the Southern prisons.

Above: Confederate prisoners of war at Ohio's Camp Chase. Treatment in Union prisons was marginally better than in Southern camps.

Opposite: A view of Andersonville prison in 1865. Opened in February 1864 to relieve crowding at the Richmond prisons, Andersonville was planned for 10,000 prisoners. At one time it held more than 30,000. An enlightened Confederate medical investigating commission had most of the prisoners moved elsewhere by October 1864.

The Pivotal Campaigns: 1863

At the beginning of the year General Burnside told President Lincoln that he was considering retirement 'to promote the public good.' Persuaded to reconsider, Burnside made plans to dismiss several of his senior officers, including General Joseph Hooker. Instead, on January 25, Lincoln relieved Burnside and appointed Hooker general in chief of the Army of the Potomac.

Hooker began preparations for a spring campaign against Lee, building his army through the winter to more than 130,000, greater than twice the size of Lee's force encamped across the Rappahannock at Fredericksburg. On April 27 Hooker marched 70,000 of his men up the Rappahannock, then across that river and the Rapidan and back toward Chancellorsville, Virginia, planning to trap Lee between this main force and the 30,000 Union soldiers under General John Sedgwick who were stationed near Fredericksburg.

On May 2, as Hooker paused in an area of dense underbrush known as the Wilderness, Lee sent General Stonewall Jackson's corps against Hooker's exposed right flank while Lee held the left in check. In what many consider to be Lee's greatest victory, as well as one of the world's classic battles, Lee and Jackson so mauled Hooker's force that the demoralized Union general withdrew the whole Army of the Potomac back across the Rappahannock, thus ending another massive, ill-conducted Federal offensive. But, while regrouping on the evening of May 2, Jackson had been wounded in the arm by his own troops. Lee's irreplaceable general died a week later, Jeb Stuart, Lee's cavalry chief, briefly taking Jackson's command. Casualties were high on both sides; Hooker lost about 17,000 and Lee 13,000 men.

Meanwhile, in the West, General Grant had been trying a number of ways to take Vicksburg, Mississippi, the last major Confederate port on the Mississippi River. Vicksburg's fall would open the river to Union shipping and divide the Confederacy. So frustrated was Grant in his attempts to find a way to get at this 'Gibraltar of the Confederacy' that he even briefly considered a frontal attack from the west. He decided instead on a more complex plan to take the fortress. First Grant would march and float his men through wet bottomlands west of the river to a point below Vicksburg. At night, Admiral David Dixon Porter would run supply boats and empty transports past the batteries, meet Grant, and carry his force across to the east bank. Meanwhile, to the north of the city, General Sherman would create a diversion, moving his men up and down the river to draw the attention of the Confederates under General John C. Pemberton away from Grant's maneuver.

The plan worked perfectly, and Grant crossed the Mississippi on April 30 with no resistance. Against orders, Grant moved east toward Jackson, Mississippi, where General Joseph E. Johnston was gathering reinforcements for Vicksburg. Grant took the town quickly on May 14 and then turned west to meet Pemberton, who had been searching for Grant's nonexistent supply line. Hard fighting at Champion's Hill and Big Black River on May 16 and 17 forced Pemberton's 30,000 Confederates to withdraw to Vicksburg, where they were trapped.

Grant mounted several frontal assaults, but the fortress held, and Grant settled in for the siege he had hoped to avoid. Pemberton surrendered on July 4, after Vicksburg's citizens and soldiers had been reduced to eating mules and peas and various vermin. This decisive Union victory took a large Rebel army out of the conflict and created in Grant a new national hero.

After his success at Chancellorsville in May, Lee moved north from the Fredericksburg area toward Pennsylvania, where he planned to feed his undersupplied army on the state's rich farmlands. Lee's object was to force the Army of the Potomac into a great battle that would either destroy it or so weaken it that he would be free to divert forces from the East to deal with the growing threat in the West.

On June 10 Confederate General Ewell's II Corps left Culpeper, Virginia, moving northwest. By mid-June he was joined by A. P. Hill and James Longstreet. General Joseph Hooker, at the head of the Union Army of the Potomac, correctly interpreted Lee's movements and moved to intercept him, despite harrassment from Jeb Stuart's cavalry. By June 28 Lee's army was in Pennsylvania, headed for the state capital at Harrisburg. On that day Lincoln, doubting Hooker's ability, replaced him with General George G. Meade.

Learning of Meade's continued northward movement, Lee collected his scattered forces near Gettysburg, and early on July 1 units of opposing cavalry made contact. Ewell, Hill, and Longstreet then forced a Federal corps under O. O. Howard out of the town and into the fishhook-shaped range of hills that lay to its south. With the arrival of more of Meade's force, the Federals quickly entrenched themselves on Culp's Hill, Cemetery Hill, and along Cemetery Ridge. On the second day of the Battle of Gettysburg the Union continued to control the heights, despite major assaults from Longstreet and Hill. On July 3 Lee, over Longstreet's objections, determined to attack the Federal center. Commanded by Longstreet, 15,000 Confederate infantry charged across open ground and were torn apart by Union rifle and artillery fire. The campaign ended the next day, on July 4, as Lee took his gutted Confederate Army of Northern Virginia back toward his home state.

Poor weather hampered Meade's cautious pursuit, and in ten days Lee recrossed the Potomac. He had lost 28,000 men, which the depleted South could no longer replace. In combination with the surrender of Vicksburg that same day, the Confederate withdrawal from Gettysburg marked the turning point of the war. The North could now sense final victory; the invasion of Pennsylvania would be the South's last major offensive.

In the West, after Murfreesboro, Confederate General Braxton Bragg had established a defensive line in central Tennessee in January 1863. In late June, Union General Rosecrans had resumed his offensive against Bragg, forcing him first to Chattanooga and then, early in September, into northwestern Georgia. Pursuing what they believed to be a retreating army, the Federals found themselves dispersed across 40 miles of mountains. Sensing a trap, Rosecrans regrouped his forces along Chickamauga Creek where, on September 19, fighting erupted between a reconnoitering Union division under George H. Thomas and Nathan B. Forrest's cavalry. In a day of fierce fighting in which Bragg attempted to cut Rosecrans off from Chattanooga, losses were huge but little was gained. Rosecrans had succeeded in establishing a good defensive position, but on the next day Longstreet, who had come from Virginia to reinforce Bragg, charged into an inadvertent gap in the Union lines and split the Federal force in two, precipitating a disorderly Union retreat with thousands of casualties. But while Rosecrans fled to Chattanooga, Thomas was able to hold the left flank long enough to save the army from disaster. Then he withdrew to join Rosecrans. Each side had lost more than a quarter of its strength in this costliest two-day battle of the war.

Besieged by Bragg, who was established in strong positions on Orchard Knob, Lookout Mountain, and Missionary Ridge, the Union army in Chattanooga was now placed under the command of General Thomas, the 'Rock of Chickamauga.' Toward the end of October, Grant (now in charge of the entire area between the Mississippi and the eastern mountains) arrived, and soon the Federal troops were resupplied. By mid-November, Joseph Hooker, with two corps from Virginia, and William Tecumseh Sherman, with a corps from Vicksburg, had joined Grant and Thomas.

On November 23 some 20,000 Union soldiers suddenly attacked the Rebel positions, capturing Orchard Knob, the hill between Missionary Ridge and Chatanooga. On the next day Hooker easily took Lookout Mountain in the 'Battle Above the Clouds,' and on the following day the entire Union army moved on Missionary Ridge. With Sherman forcing the north end and Hooker the right, Grant directed Thomas's men to take the center. Driving the Confederate troops before them, they ignored orders to stop halfway up the steep slope to reorganize and continued their rush up the hill to drive the Rebels in panic from the crest. Bragg retreated to Dalton, Georgia. The Union was now in position to launch an invasion into the heart of the Deep South.

As the armies moved into winter quarters, the Confederacy looked back on a year of major setbacks, while the Union made plans for final victory.

Left: Union General Daniel E. Sickles fought in the Peninsular Campaign, at Chancellorsville, and at Gettysburg, where he lost a leg when his corps withstood a charge on the Federal left.

Above: A Currier and Ives lithograph shows an imaginary Union advance on faltering Rebels at Chancellorsville on May 3, 1868. In fact, by the 3rd Lee had all but won the battle.

Splendid Advance of Sykes's Regulars.

Centre of our Line of Battle

Steam-Mill used as a Medical Depot.

THE BATTLES AT CHANCELLORSVILLE.—From Sketches by Mr. A. R. Waud.—[See Page 881.]

Left: Three views of Chancellorsville from sketches by A. R. Waud. At the top, an advance by Union troops; in the center, the Federal line of battle; at the bottom, a lumber mill used as a medical station.

Opposite: The wounding of Stonewall Jackson at Chancellorsville on May 2. He died of complications from the wound one week later, a severe loss to Lee and to the Confederacy.

Above: Men of the Stonewall Brigade cheer General Jackson as they hurry towards Chancellorsville. After the death of Stonewall Jackson, his old unit was allowed to continue to use the name through its campaigns.

Right: The last meeting of General Robert E. Lee and Stonewall Jackson. Together they planned every movement at Chancellorsville, and on Jackson's death, Lee said, 'I know not how to replace him.'

Above: Union General Joseph Hooker commanded the Army of the Potomac at Chancellorsville. Twice the size of Lee's army, the Union force was surprised by Jackson's flank attack and was forced to withdraw.

Right: Engraving from a sketch by field artist J. Becker shows the 14th New York Infantry encamped behind a breastwork in the Wilderness on the night of May 6, awaiting orders to move back across the Rappahannock.

Opposite: Two views of the Battle of Chancellorsville by artist A. R. Waud. At the top, the Union 2nd and 3rd Corps facing Jackson's assault; at the bottom, General Hooker's field headquarters.

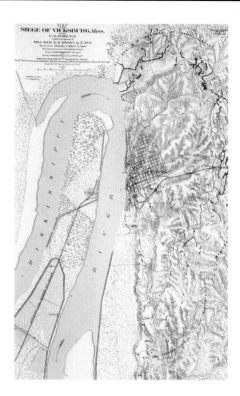

Above: U.S. Army map of the siege of Vicksburg, showing the Federal (blue) and Rebel (red) positions. Grant's 47-day siege ended on July 4, 1863, with a Confederate surrender.

Right: General A. P. Hovey's Union artillery battery firing shells into Vicksburg during the siege.

Left: General Grant, sketched at his field headquarters on July 3 as he read Confederate General John C. Pemberton's terms for the surrender of Vicksburg.

Below: Vicksburg's defenders fire down on Union troops trapped in a crater made by an exploding mine at the end of a trench that had been run to a position near the Rebel lines.

IMPORTANT FROM AMERICA!!
Awful Slaughter at Vicksburg,
And Elsewhere,
The Bloody Conflict between the North & South
CONTINUED!

We regret to say that this unnatural war seems still to rush upon the unhappy Yanky with fearful impetuosity, so as to stun the entire population and saturate the States of America with blood, by sacrificing

well. They suffered terribly, for out of a regiment of 900, 600 were killed or wounded in an hour!

The Prize Court at Key West has laid down the law of confiscation so as to in-

demned at the rate of two each week."

Although 49,688 emigrants had arrived in New York from Ireland since the first of January, 1863, and though the negroes are said to be the " best-hope

line of works between the outer line opposed to us and the city. While the charge was being made on the 22nd arms of our sharpshooters, posted in the trees overlooking the fortifications, could plainly see contrabands and white men digging for dear life.

OUR LOSSES

I regret to learn that Colonel Abbot, of the 30th Iowa, was killed on the 22nd instant. He was a brave officer, and his loss is universally regretted. In the battle of Champion's Hill, on the 16th in-

that the Government will find in the Negroes effective supporters.

General Banks' loss from the 23rd to the 30th ult., was 1,000 men, including many of his ablest officers.

General Sherman has died of his wounds.

General Neal Dow is also dangerously wounded.

Above: Europe watched the Civil War intently. This Irish paper describes events of mid-June at Vicksburg.

Right: A street view of Vicksburg, Mississippi. The town was fortified by the Confederates in 1862, after the fall of Fort Donelson, in order to close the Mississippi to Union shipping.

Left: Union Battery Sherman at the siege of Vicksburg.

Below: Under steady Federal bombardment the people of Vicksburg went into caves and underground. Surrender came on July 4 as supplies were almost exhausted.

Right: Admiral David Dixon Porter's fleet of gunboats and transports running the Confederate batteries at Vicksburg on April 16. Only one ship was lost.

Right below: Vicksburg. Grant was able to circumvent its formidable defenses by combining the use of his land and naval forces.

Far right: Admiral David Dixon Porter, commander of the Federal Mississippi Squadron, became superintendent of the U.S. Naval Academy after the war.

Opposite: A depiction of Pemberton's surrender to General Grant on July 4, which ended the siege of Vicksburg. The surrender of Port Hudson, Louisiana, a few days later, brought the entire Mississippi River under Federal control.

Above: On the last day of fighting at Gettysburg, July 3, Confederate prisoners are led off from the front lines. Lee gambled 15,000 men in a frontal assault – later known as 'Pickett's Charge' – against Meade's center. The gamble was lost, and Lee retreated to Virginia.

Right: Confederate General Ambrose P. Hill. An encounter between a corps of his cavalry and Union Cavalry on the morning of July 1 initiated the battle at Gettysburg. Two days later his men would provide most of the final assault force launched against Meade's army.

Left: Union generals Daniel E. Sickles (left) and George G. Meade on July 3. When Sickles moved without orders to a new position in a peach orchard, he was badly wounded, and his corps was scattered.

Above: Views of Gettysburg: Federal artillery firing at close range (top) and leaving the field (bottom).

Above: General Robert E. Lee in 1864. Lee had wanted a decisive victory in the North.

Above right: Sketch by A. R. Waud of the death of Union General John Reynolds on the morning of July 1.

Right Lincoln at the dedication of the cemetery at Gettysburg on November 19, 1863. His brief Gettysburg Address received merely a polite reception.

Left: Photograph by Timothy O'Sullivan, one of Mathew Brady's crew, of Union dead in a field at Gettysburg: they had been stripped of their valuable shoes. By invading Pennsylvania, Lee had hoped to force the Union into a battle that would either win the war for the South at a stroke or leave the Army of the Potomac so weakened that it could not prevent the South from diverting troops from Virginia to deal with the mounting threat in the West. But Southern casualties at Gettysburg were so high that it was Lee's Army of Northern Virginia that was now fatally weakened. It would thereafter be unable either to mount any important offensives in the East or to contribute significantly to the war in the Western Theater.

Right: The third and final day of fighting at Gettysburg, July 3, 1863. Union troops withstood Lee's frontal assault, and the campaign was ended. The Confederates lost about 3900 killed, 18,700 wounded, and 5400 missing, a total of 28,000, or more than a third of their force. The Union, out of a somewhat larger force of 88,000, lost about 3150 killed, 14,500 wounded, and 5350 missing, a total of 23,000.

Address delivered at the dedication of the Cemetery at Gettysburg.

Four score and seven years ago our fathers brought forth on this continent, a new nation, conceived in Liberty, and dedicated to the proposition that all men are created equal.

Now we are engaged in a great civil war, testing whether that nation, or any nation so conceived and so dedicated, can long endure. We are met on a great battle-field of that war. We have come to dedicate a portion of that field, as a final resting place for those who here gave their lives, that that nation might live. It is altogether fitting and proper that we should do this.

But, in a larger sense, we can not dedicate— we can not consecrate— we can not hallow— this ground. The brave men, living and dead, who struggled here, have consecrated it, far above our poor power to add or detract. The world will little note, nor long remember what we say here, but it can never forget what they did here. It is for us the living, rather, to be dedicated here to the unfinished work which they who fought here have thus far so nobly advanced. It is rather for us to be here dedicated to the great task remaining before us— that from these honored dead we take increased devotion to that cause for which they gave the last full measure of devotion— that we here highly resolve that these dead shall not have died in vain— that this nation, under God, shall have a new birth of freedom— and that government of the people, by the people, for the people, shall not perish from the earth.

Abraham Lincoln.

November 19. 1863.

Top: A Timothy O'Sullivan photograph of part of the battlefield as seen from Cemetery Hill.

Above: A copy of Lincoln's Gettysburg Address.

Right: Lee in battle. The general preferred the uniform of a cavalry colonel. His legendary horse Traveller carried him through all of his military campaigns.

Left: General Grant (foreground) and his staff on Lookout Mountain after its capture by General Hooker on November 24, 1863. The next day, at the Battle of Missionary Ridge, Grant would put an end to a campaign in Tennessee that had begun with a Union defeat at the Battle of Chickamauga in September and had seen the Union army holed up in Chattanooga under siege for more than a month. But with his victories at Lookout Mountain and Missionary Ridge, Grant would at last open the way for the long-anticipated Union invasion of the Deep South.

Opposite top: Confederate General John Bell Hood lost the use of an arm at Gettysburg. At Chickamauga in September he was wounded in the right leg, which was amputated. Nevertheless, he continued in command through 1864.

Opposite bottom: Union pickets near Chattanooga being approached by camouflaged Rebels.

Opposite bottom right: View of the top of Missionary Ridge. Here, on November 25, General Thomas's Federal troops overran line after line of Rebel defenses and captured the crest, suddenly ending the battle.

Left: A painting commemorating the Union success at Lookout Mountain on November 24. The fighting on the fog-covered slope had been very light, and the North welcomed the victory all the more.

Above: General Thomas's men swarm over the Confederate defenders on Missionary Ridge. In the face of heavy fire, the Union attackers disregarded orders to pause and regroup, instead charging quickly to the top.

Right: The Battle Above the Clouds on Lookout Mountain. Grant had first planned to ignore Lookout Mountain but changed his mind, sending Joseph Hooker's superior force against the outnumbered Confederates.

Left: Chattanooga, Tennessee, with Lookout Mountain in the distance. The Chickamauga and Chattanooga National Military Park, with a unit here and in northeastern Georgia, is among the most thoroughly surveyed battlefields in the world.

Below: The Confederate line of battle in the Chickamauga woods.

Opposite: A wash drawing by A. R. Waud on September 19 or 20 at Chickamauga, showing part of the Union line that faced the Confederates along a six-mile front.

Right: Lookout Mountain as seen from Chattanooga. An encampment of U.S. Army engineers is in the foreground.

The Home Fronts

President Lincoln had demonstrated keen political judgment in his conduct of military affairs – directing strategy, replacing commanding generals, and marshaling the North's manpower and industrial capacity for war until a Union victory was all but inevitable. However, within Lincoln's own cabinet, as well as in his own party in Congress, were Radical Republicans who considered him too moderate in his views on emancipation, recruitment of blacks into the army, and the property and citizenship rights of the Rebels.

Men such as his able secretary of war, Edwin M. Stanton, worked with the leading Radicals in Congress – Charles Sumner in the Senate and Thaddeus Stevens in the House – to promote the idea that the secessionists had lost *all* their rights under the Constitution. Senator Benjamin Wade, an uncompromising abolitionist, chaired a meddlesome and powerful Joint Committee on the Conduct of the War. And both Lincoln's adept secretary of state, William Henry Seward, and his innovative secretary of the treasury, Salmon P. Chase, supported the Radical cause.

Outside the party, Copperheads, or Peace Democrats – Northern opponents of the war, strongest in the Midwest – argued for a reunion of North and South by negotiation, opposing emancipation, conscription, and Lincoln's wartime curtailment of certain civil liberties. From the regular Democrats – who thought Republicans could not achieve union – and from the partisan press came assaults on Lincoln's intelligence and character, and even from the War Democrats there was continued opposition to the abolition of slavery.

To finance the war Lincoln relied on Secretary of the Treasury Chase, who oversaw raising and using new taxes, borrowing great sums of money, printing paper currency, and establishing a national banking system. His chief financial agent was banker Jay Cooke, who was commissioned to raise funds for the government through private loans and bond sales.

Until he found the commander he needed in Ulysses S. Grant, Lincoln, as commander in chief, interfered readily in his generals' campaigns. But in addition to the reluctant fighters and weak strategists whom he felt free to replace, Lincoln had his share of political generals – men like Ben Butler, John C. Frémont, and Nathaniel Banks – who were poor commanders but who had such strong personal constituencies that Lincoln was obliged to retain them.

Jefferson Davis, too, had his critics, perhaps even more hostile and obstructionist than Lincoln's. He found it difficult to retain a cabinet (he had six heads of the war department), many of his best nominees preferring military duty. Only Judah P. Benjamin had his full confidence, while men like Vice President Alexander H. Stephens actively opposed his conduct of the war. The Confederate Congress was weak, ineffective, distant from the people, and bitterly divided between Davis' supporters and opponents. Senator Louis T. Wigfall may have typified those who, when not drunk or brawling among themselves, endlessly meddled with details.

Davis himself was rigid, tactless, uncommunicative, a poor administrator, and a man wrongly persuaded of his own military talent. Whereas Lincoln generally intervened to replace poor generals, Davis was all too capable of replacing good ones. The much-respected commander of the Army of Tennessee, Joseph E. Johnston, for example, he replaced with John Bell Hood, a man clearly more suited to a subordinate position. The timing could hardly have been worse, for Sherman was then closing in on Atlanta.

While the economy of the North grew under the demands of war, the blockaded South could barely keep itself supplied with munitions; manufactured goods were increasingly scarce, and the transportation system was decaying. With a weakened infrastructure, the Confederacy found it necessary to finance its war effort by printing money. About three-fifths of its income came from this source – fueling inflation and destroying investor confidence – and most of the rest from loans. Barely one percent was raised through new taxes, apparently from fear of creating disloyalty.

At its height, the entire value of Southern industrial production during the war was eclipsed by that of single Northern states such as New York, Pennsylvania, or Massachusetts. In the North military contractors and farmers prospered and, although inflation caused real wages to go down by a third, Northern inflation was relatively small compared to the skyrocketing prices in the South (flour at $1000 a barrel in 1865). To the extent that the enormous industrial expansion in the North created a labor shortage, it was largely offset by immigration. In the South the acute shortage of manpower found no such relief.

Government spending and high tariffs fueled the Northern economic boom, and government policy promoted internal improvements such as Western settlement under the Homestead Act of 1862 and development of the transcontinental railroads, which in 1862 received generous land grants and loans to complete the spanning of the continent. In fact, the flow of commerce during the war saw a fundamental shift from the north-to-south of river traffic to the east-to-west of rail traffic serving the ports of the Northeast.

A major problem for the South was its inability to distribute goods. Acceptance by Europe of the Union blockade of Southern ports had caused many farmers to shift from cotton and tobacco export crops to foodcrops. Nevertheless, civilians and soldiers often went hungry because these crops were not being delivered. Also, foraging by Southern soldiers and by invading armies decimated the countryside.

The main goal of Federal diplomacy during the war was to maintain British and French neutrality, whereas the Confederacy looked to the European powers for recognition of its independence. Early in the war the British had considered recognition but decided to await a decisive Southern victory, which never arrived. The Confederate theory that English and French dependency on Southern cotton would bring intervention proved to be only that. In practice, not only were European warehouses full of cotton but alternate sources had become available, and at the same time Northern products and markets remained important to Europe.

Although British shipbuilders contracted with the Confederacy to construct commerce raiders such as the cruisers *Florida, Alabama,* and *Shenandoah,* as well as several ironclad rams, only once did the Union and Britain come close to a direct clash. This was during the famous *Trent* affair. On November 8, 1861, Captain Charles Wilkes of USS *San Jacinto* forcibly removed Confederates James M. Mason, agent to England, and John Slidell, agent to France, from the British steamship *Trent*, bound for England from Bermuda. The two were imprisoned in Boston. The British government demanded redress for this violation of international law, threatening war. Although his decision was unpopular at home, Lincoln acceded to British demands for the release of Mason and Slidell, and they were allowed in January to continue their voyage.

In January 1865 Congress adopted the Thirteenth Amendment abolishing slavery in the United States. In his determination to preserve the Union, Lincoln had pledged not to interfere with slavery where it already existed and to uphold the rights of Southerners. However, pressure from the Radicals and from military requirements, as well as his desire to influence European opinion, moved him to prepare an executive order abolishing slavery in the Confederacy. To avoid the appearance of weakness, Secretary Seward persuaded Lincoln to postpone the order until the Union could claim a significant battlefield victory. Thus the preliminary announcement was delayed until September 22, 1862, after the Battle of Antietam. The final Emancipation Proclamation followed 100 days later, on January 1, 1863.

With so much of the population involved in the war, government policies and military activities were of considerable general concern. To satisfy the public's demand for news, hundreds of newspaper correspondents were sent into the field. Their thorough coverage was sometimes viewed as troublesome by the military; Halleck, McClellan, Sherman, and Meade frequently imposed censorship, although Grant and Lee, understanding the need to maintain public support for the war effort, usually cooperated with newsmen. Field artists and photographers were also given ready access to the battlefield. In Washington, however, a free wartime press presented problems for some, and a number of papers were temporarily shut down after printing critical editorials considered disloyal. But such cases were exceptional. In general, the administration's relations with the press were relaxed, and that doubtless contributed much to the fact that the Civil War was reported in greater detail and more objectively than any previous war in history.

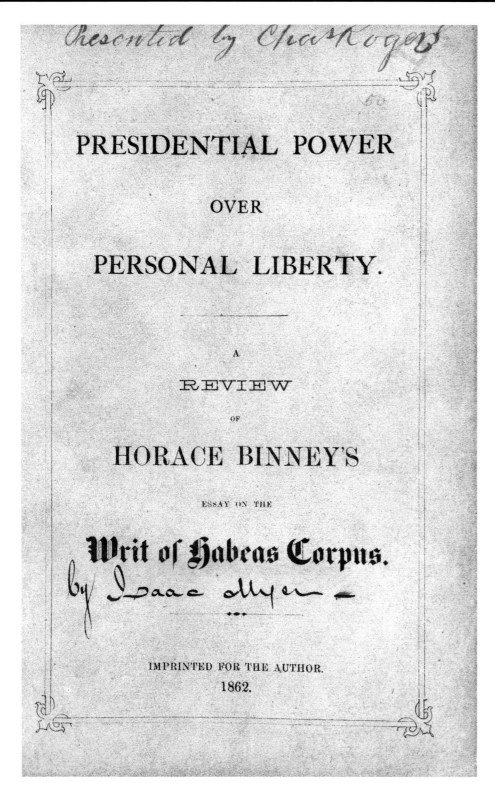

Presented by Chas Rogers

PRESIDENTIAL POWER

OVER

PERSONAL LIBERTY.

A

REVIEW

OF

HORACE BINNEY'S

ESSAY ON THE

Writ of Habeas Corpus.

by Isaac Myer

IMPRINTED FOR THE AUTHOR.
1862.

B-19

Left: William H. Seward, seen here with his daughter in a Mathew Brady photo, was President Lincoln's secretary of state. An extremely able statesman, he joined the Cabinet thinking he could dominate the president, who soon made him into a loyal supporter.

Far left: An essay in rebuttal of a legal defense of Lincoln's suspension (1861) of the writ of habeas corpus in the North (so that disloyal persons might be held without trial). That defense, by lawyer Horace Binney, raised a storm of protest, and more than 40 separate replies were published.

Left: Union General Benjamin F. Butler had been a Massachusetts politician until appointed a major general of militia in 1861. A failure as a field commander, he was made governor of New Orleans after its capture by Admiral Farragut, but he so angered local citizens that he was removed.

Opposite: Lincoln (5) and Davis (6) each had problems with some Cabinet members and senior officers. Salmon P. Chase (3, and at left) and William H. Seward (4) sided with the Radicals in Congress. Vice President Alexander H. Stephens (7) was opposed to secession and often criticized Davis' conduct of the war. Lincoln considered several of his generals to be ineffective, and Davis expressed open dislike for some of his. Other figures in the painting are: Benjamin (8), Ewell (13), Price (14), Hood (15), Stuart (16), Bragg (17), Buckner (18), Breckinridge (19), Pemberton (20), Kearney (21), Blair (22), Stoneman (23), Slocum (24), McPherson (25), Logan (26), Howard (33), Burnside (34), Siegal (35), Rosecrans (36), Sherman (37), Thomas (38), Grant (39), Meade (40), J. E. Johnston (41), R. E. Lee (42) Beauregard (43), Longstreet (44), Hampton (45), Hill (36), Forrest (47), Jackson (48).

Left: Secretary of the Treasury Salmon P. Chase was politically disloyal to Lincoln at virtually every turn, yet the president appointed him to be chief justice of the Supreme Court when Roger Taney died in 1864.

Right: Confederate paper money. To help finance its war effort, the Confederacy had to print money; about 60 percent of its income came from that source. The twenty-dollar note promises to pay on demand; the fifty-dollar note carries a pledge to pay that amount two years after ratification of a peace treaty between the belligerents.

Left: General Joseph E. Johnston was disliked by Jefferson Davis. Despite his recognized abilities as a soldier, Johnston was replaced by John Bell Hood, a less commanding leader.

Below: Judah P. Benjamin was the only man in the Cabinet with Davis' complete confidence. He became secretary of state after having held several other Cabinet posts.

Opposite: Jefferson Davis meeting with his Cabinet and General Lee. Only three of fourteen of his Cabinet members remained with him throughout the war. General Lee had to tolerate Davis' frequent interference in military matters.

Right: Alexander H. Stephens became vice president of the Confederate States of America even though he had voted against secession in the Georgia convention in 1861. He opposed granting Jefferson Davis extraordinary war powers and was a constant critic of the manner in which the president conducted the war.

Right: A railroad company broadside encourages western settlement. The Homestead Act of 1862 and the prewar land grants for railroad development helped to fuel an immense growth in population and industry. By 1860 the North had twice the population of the South, and twice the railroad track, and showed the potential to be a world-class manufacturing region.

Ho! For the New Kansas.

We invite the attention of all who are contemplating a change of location, or who want

A FARM OR HOME IN THE WEST

TO THE SPECIAL ADVANTAGES OF THE

LANDS

OF THE

ATCHISON, TOPEKA AND SANTA FE R. R.

SITUATED ALONG THE BEAUTIFUL

COTTONWOOD AND ARKANSAS VALLEYS, THROUGH SOUTH-WESTERN KANSAS.

FIRST.—It is a NEW COUNTRY, recently opened for settlement by the building of the Atchison, Topeka and Santa Fe Railroad.

SECOND.—For its CHOICE CLIMATE. In latitude 38 north, the latitude of Central Kentucky and Virginia, RICH SOIL, and abundance of PURE WATER.

THIRD.—The large proportion of VALLEY LAND.

FOURTH.—HEALTH. Its altitude 1,000 to 3,000 feet above the level of the sea, a porous subsoil and well drained surface, no stagnant water or overflowed lands, alone tell the story of its HEALTHFUL CLIMATE.

FIFTH.—Its rapid settlement, unprecedented in the history of the West, with the cream of Eastern immigration, has given it prosperous churches, schools, mills, and the conveniences of a well settled community.

SIXTH.—By the 1st of November, 1875, the A. T. & S. F. R. R. will be COMPLETED TO PUEBLO, COLORADO, there connecting with the Rocky Mountain system of railroads, and, as Kansas is the nearest Agricultural State, her products will find a ready and profitable market in the extensive mineral regions developed by the extension of this road.

SEVENTH.—With all other advantages we offer our lands at the LOWEST PRICES and on the MOST FAVORABLE TERMS of any Land Grant in the West.

The Cottonwood and Arkansas Valleys are destined to become densely settled—the homes of rich and prosperous communities.

STOCK RAISING.

The abundance of excellent water in SPRINGS and RUNNING STREAMS, combined with CHEAP LAND of superior quality, covered with nutritious grasses, and the finest climate in the world, makes it the finest stock country in the West.

In selecting a new HOME, cast your fortune with a GREAT ENTERPRISE like the **Atchison, Topeka and Santa Fe Railroad,** which is destined to be the favorite thoroughfare across the Continent.

Everyone seeking a NEW HOME should, by all means, visit our lands before locating.

TERMS OF SALE:

TERMS NO. 1—Is on eleven years' time, with seven per cent. interest. One-tenth of purchase money paid down at time of purchase, and one year's interest on the remainder. The next two years, only interest payments. Afterwards, one-tenth of the principal, and interest on the remainder annually, until the contract is paid out.

TERMS NO. 2—Is on eleven years' time, with only the interest, at seven per cent. for the first four years. After that time, one-eighth of the principal, and interest on the remainder annually until the expiration of the contract.

TERMS NO. 3—Are our Short Credit terms, where, in consideration of the purchaser paying one-third of the principal, and ten per cent. interest on the remainder, and the balance in one and two years, we make a discount of TWENTY per cent. from the price.

TERMS NO. 4—Is a cash sale, where we make a discount of TWENTY per cent. from the appraised value.

For full particulars, and any special information desired, address,

A. S. JOHNSON,
Acting Land Commissioner for the A. T. & S. F. R. R. Co.,
TOPEKA, KANSAS.

Left: Immigrants arrived by the tens of thousands in the North; the South had little immigration. Here, newly arrived Irish and German immigrants in New York are offered bounties to enlist in the Union army. During the war the flow of immigrants somewhat slowed but never ceased.

Left below: A Union rail yard, part of the huge military supply depot at City Point, Virginia. In addition to a rail line to the front, this testament to Northern strength boasted a mile of wharves along its shoreline.

Above: After the capture of New Bern, North Carolina, by General Burnside in 1862, the army distributed captured clothing to the needy inhabitants.

Right: After the fall of Richmond, April 1865. This leading manufacturing center of the South saw its industries destroyed, under government orders, by the evacuating Rebel garrison.

Left: In a cartoon entitled 'Cotton in the Stocks,' a figure representing France demands of the South whether its refusal to export cotton is an attempt to exact French intervention in the war. The Confederate attempt failed because both France and England had good supplies on hand and were developing alternate sources. Cotton, it could be said, 'was no longer king.'

Above: A Southern family evacuates a war area. The total war that was waged by the Union army beginning in September 1864 exacted a terrible toll in lives and devastated property. Grant's goal was to destroy the South's economic capacity for continuing the war. Siege warfare, directed at garrisons occupying cities, also took its toll of civilian residents.

Right: In order to build a navy, the Confederacy sought aid from abroad, contracting with British shipyards for the constructon of a fleet of 18 cruisers. The most famous of these, CSS *Alabama*, is shown being sunk off Cherbourg, France, by the frigate USS *Kearsarge* on June 19, 1864. CSS *Alabama* alone had taken 70 prizes, and after the war the United States made claims against Britain for damages to merchant shipping done by *Alabama* and other Confederate cruisers.

Above: USS *San Jacinto* halts the British steam packet *Trent* in open waters on November 8, 1861, as it departs for England from Bermuda carrying two Southern agents. The removal of the two men – James Mason and John Slidell – and their imprisonment in Boston sparked an exchange that brought the Union and Britain close to war.

Left: A group of foreign observers at Camp Winfield Scott near Yorktown, Virginia, May 1862. At this time the British were considering recognition of the Confederacy, which likely would have meant independence for the South. When General Lee withdrew to Virginia after being stymied at Antietam, the British and French chose not to grant recognition to the CSA.

Above: A camp of 'contrabands' at Richmond. Because slaves were property they were referred to as contrabands when taken from their owners by Union armies. At first employed as laborers, they were soon guarding their own camps and wearing cast-off uniforms, and by July 1862 freed Southern blacks were actively being recruited for the Union army.

Right: Guard detail of the 107th US Colored Infantry at Fort Corcoran, near Washington, D.C. Following the Emancipation Proclamation recruitment of blacks into the Union army grew at a rapidly accelerating pace.

Left: Picket station manned by black soldiers at Dutch Gap, Virginia, in November 1864. By that time, black troops had demonstrated their fighting abilities in several major campaigns.

Above: Mustering out of black troops at Little Rock, Arkansas, April 1865: an engraving for *Harper's Weekly*. About 186,000 black soldiers had served in 120 infantry, 13 artillery, and 7 cavalry regiments.

Right: As enthusiasm for enlistment waned, both North and South passed conscription laws. The advertisement is by a broker who specialized in securing substitutes for drafted men. In the North, a man could also avoid service by paying a commutation fee. Although the North had far greater reserves of manpower than the South, it too had difficulty in keeping up with the attrition of its armies. In relation to total population, war-related deaths in the Civil War were about eight times higher than those suffered by America in World War II.

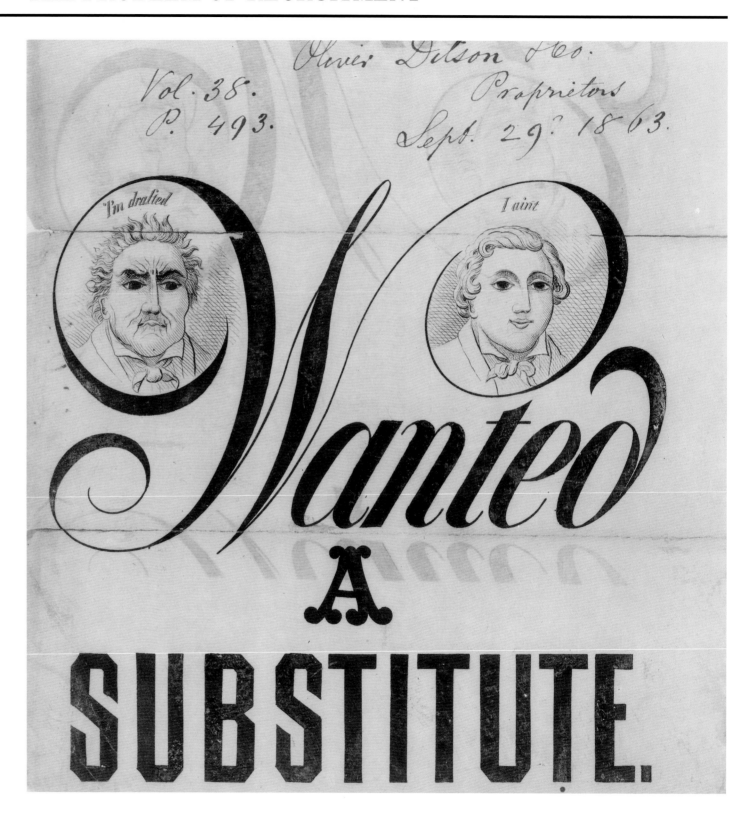

Left: A recruiting poster entitled 'Come and Join Us Brother,' published in Philadelphia by the Committee for Recruiting Colored Regiments.

Above: The draft was neither popular nor very successful, and was sometimes resisted violently. The draft riots in New York City in July 13-16, 1863, were the most notable protests; more than 400 people died.

FREEMEN!
AVOID CONSCRIPTION!

The undersigned desires to raise a Company for the Confederate States service, and for that purpose I call upon the people of the Counties of Jefferson and Hawkins, Tenn., to meet promptly at Russellville, on SATURDAY, JULY 19th, 1862, and organize a Company.

By so doing you will avoid being taken as Conscripts, for that Act will now be enforced by order of the War Department. Rally, then, my Countrymen, to your Country's call.

S. M. DENNISON,
Of the Confederate States Army.

CHARLESTON, Tenn., JUNE 30, 1862.

Above: In the face of mounting battle losses the Confederacy found it necessary to institute a draft in April 1862. Volunteer companies were preferred, however, and individuals still sought to raise their own units.

Right: An enthusiastic 1861 lithograph shows departing Union soldiers at a 'Volunteer Refreshment Saloon, Supported Gratuitously by the Citizens of Philadelphia.' The first year of the war saw a great burst of volunteerism.

Above: From the *Confederate War Etchings* of Southern propagandist Adalbert Volck comes this cartoon savaging Northern recruitment policy. The young man is being offered a substitute from a 'supply of able bodied men.'

THE HOUSE-TOPS IN CHARLESTON DURING THE BOMBARDMENT OF SUMTER.

Above: Horace Greeley published the New York *Tribune* from 1841 until his death in 1872. He did not trust the president, nor did Lincoln trust him. During the war his editorial policies were inconsistent. He at first held with the Radical Republicans, but in the end he advocated 'universal amnesty and impartial suffrage' in the South.

Right: Engravings of works by artists in the field appeared regularly in *Harper's Weekly, Leslie's Illustrated Newspaper*, and other publications. The bombardment of Fort Sumter as seen from the roofs of Charleston filled *Harper's* front page. A notice inside promised more pictures from artists in both the North and South.

Left: Transportable headquarters of the New York *Herald* in the field. Many soldiers viewed as meddlesome the probing efforts of the hundreds of reporters of the new popular press. Both Grant and Lee, however, appreciated the public's need to be informed if it was to continue to support the war efforts.

Right: Mathew Brady (in straw hat) with a battery of Federal artillery at Petersburg in June 1864.

Below: A crew of Brady's photographers with portable darkroom at their camp at Petersburg.

Below right: A Brady photograph of field artist Alfred R. Waud at the Gettysburg battlefield.

Left: In an Alexander Gardner photo, a vendor sells newspapers near the town of Culpeper, Virginia, in November 1863. No previous war had ever been as thoroughly or speedily reported as was this war. The sheer volume of information about it fascinated contemporary readers and continues to fascinate their descendants.

Right: The detective Allan Pinkerton (seated, right) at General McClellan's headquarters at Antietam. Under the name E. J. Allen he provided the general with often exaggerated reports of Confederate strength. Pinkerton left the army after McClellan was relieved of his command in November 1862. Both the North and the South often had to plan their military operations using inadequate intelligence information about enemy strengths and movements. Stonewall Jackson was exceptional in his ability to gather and correctly analyze data of this sort.

Above: Confederate spy Belle Boyd was imprisoned twice for gathering information from Union officers and passing it to Rebels in Virginia. After the war she appeared on the stage as an actress. She also lectured on her wartime experiences.

Right: Union Colonel Lafayette C. Baker headed the North's wartime secret service.

Above: Taking advantage of Lincoln's love of Shakespeare and joke-telling, the cartoonist J. H. Howard drew General McClellan, the 1864 Democratic presidential candidate, as Hamlet quoting, 'I knew him, Horatio; a fellow of infinite jest . . . where be your jibes now?'

Above right: A Thomas Nast cartoon that contributed significantly to Lincoln's reelection in 1864. 'Dedicated to the Chicago Convention' that nominated McClellan and called the war a failure, it shows a triumphant Jefferson Davis taking the hand of a beaten Union.

Right: A vicious cartoon predicts the dire consequences of the antislavery policies of Lincoln, Charles Sumner, Horace Greeley, and Henry Ward Beecher.

Published by Chas Magnus,   Volunteers at Home.   12 Frankfort St. N.Y.

We've a Million in the Field.

Written and Composed by Stephen C. Foster.
Published by S. T. Gordon, 538 Broadway.

The flags are flying
  And brave men dying,
The din of the battle is revealed;
  The Union's quaking,
  The land is shaking
With the tramp of a million in the field.

Chorus.

We've a million in the field.
  A million in the field,
While our flag is slighted
  With hearts united
We can bring a million more to the field.

We were peaceful hearted
  In days departed,
While foes kept their blighting plans concealed,
  But they now must weather
  The storms they gather,
For they must meet a million in the field.

Chorus.

Down in old Kentucky,
  They're true and plucky,
They know that the Union is their shield
  And they'll do their duty
  In all its beauty,
When they find we've a million in the field.

Chorus.

500 Illustrated Ballads, lithographed and printed by
CHARLES MAGNUS, No. 12 Frankfort Street, New York.
Branch Office: No. 520 7th St. Washington, D. C.

Left: Stephen Foster, the nation's most noteworthy composer in the period before the Civil War, composed this song in New York toward the end of his life. It is a Union call to arms which concludes with an appeal to the border state of Kentucky.

Above: Julia Ward Howe was a prominent reformer who, with her husband Samuel Gridley Howe, published the abolitionist journal *Commonwealth*. Her 'Battle Hymn of the Republic,' sung to the tune of 'John Brown's Body,' first appeared in the *Atlantic Monthly* in February 1862.

Left: Cover of 'A National Song.' Such patriotic songs were generally more popular on the home front than among the troops.

Above: Sentimental songs that spoke of love, longing, and loneliness, such as 'Tenting Tonight on the Old Camp Ground,' were hits with the soldiers.

The Naval War

At the start of the Civil War the Union had only 42 navy ships in commission; the Confederacy, of course, had none. By the end of 1864, an aggressive Federal shipbuilding program had produced some 700 warships. The South was able to build a number of ironclads and to contract with British builders for a small fleet of cruisers. The ironclads were effective nuisances, but the cruisers took an astoundingly high toll of U.S. merchant ships; so high, in fact, that insurance rates for U.S.-flag vessels forced many shipowners to register their merchantmen under foreign flags.

The ironclads were the most original of the new weapons being introduced to warfare. After the U.S. installation at Norfolk, Virginia, was destroyed to keep it from Confederate hands, the Rebels recovered the burned hulk of the frigate *Merrimac* and built a house-like, iron-covered superstructure atop her still-serviceable hull. Recommissioned as CSS *Virginia*, she was fitted with a gun at bow and stern and four on each side, and on her bow she carried a long iron ram. In the fall of 1861, John Ericsson, a Swedish engineer who had come to America, offered the Union navy his plans for an armored gun platform, a huge floating raft supporting a single rotating gun turret firing two 11-inch cannons. In October, after learning of the building of *Virginia*, the navy contracted with Ericsson for his ironclad. His *Monitor* (the name later applied to the entire class) was launched in New York only four months later.

On March 8, 1862, CSS *Virginia* entered Hampton Roads from the Elizabeth River near Norfolk. Encountering fire from Union warships, she quickly dispatched the sloop of war USS *Cumberland* with her ram and then sank the frigate USS *Congress* with explosive shells. A second frigate ran aground in its haste to flee. On the next day, in one of those odd wartime coincidences, Ericsson's *Monitor* appeared in Hampton Roads, having been towed south by tug, and the two ungainly behemoths met in inconclusive combat. Each ship took dozens of hits without serious damage; after about four hours both captains turned away. Two months later, to prevent capture by the Union, *Virginia* was scuttled at Norfolk; *Monitor* sank off Cape Hatteras in heavy seas on December 31 while returning to New York. But each of these vessels became the pattern for its own navy's ironclads, and each side began to build them as fast as they could.

Some of the new ironclads saw action in the river campaigns, notably at the Battle of New Orleans, where Confederate gunboats and fireships failed to keep Admiral Farragut from New Orleans in April 1862, and at Vicksburg a year later, where Admiral Porter's fleet of gunboat-escorted transports ran the Confederate defenses on the Mississippi.

While its participation in the land campaigns was certainly one of the most important of the Union navy's roles, its coastal blockade may have been even more effective in helping to bring the war to a close. Before General Winfield Scott retired as general in chief of the U.S. Army in 1861, he strongly advocated a naval blockade.

This plan to isolate the South became Lincoln's strategy, and by the end of the year a thin cordon had been established, first by the capture of two Rebel forts guarding Hatteras Inlet (a haven for blockade-runners), then by establishing a repair and supply base at Port Royal, South Carolina, and finally by taking and garrisoning Ship Island near the entrance to Mobile Bay.

In the following year, Confederate defenses from Roanoke, North Carolina, to New Orleans fell to the Union, and the blockade continued to be reinforced through the war. It was never completely effective, owing to the limited number of naval vessels and crews available to patrol the 3500 miles of Confederate coastline, but by the end of the war about half the ships that attempted to run the blockade were being intercepted.

There were tempting rewards for blockade-running. Goods were carried in both directions. Exported cotton was exchanged for European merchandise that was sold in the South at greatly inflated prices; a few trips yielded generous profits. All kinds of ships were used, but returning cargo would frequently be off-loaded to swifter vessels in the Caribbean – particularly in Bermuda and the Bahamas – for the dangerous run to Confederate ports.

Some blockade-runners also doubled as privateers, attacking Northern merchantmen on the high seas, but the most notorious of the commerce raiders were the 18 cruisers built in British shipyards and commissioned for that purpose. They took some 250 prizes: CSS *Alabama* accounted for about 70 of these; *Florida*, 55; and *Shenandoah*, hunting in the Pacific, 40, mostly whalers.

In an attempt to end Confederate blockade-running in the Gulf of Mexico, Admiral Farragut, on August 5, 1864, entered the narrow channel of Mobile Bay with his flagship, the frigate *Hartford*, and a mixed force of other wooden vessels, plus four ironclad monitors. The fleet fought its way past defending forts Morgan and Gaines, through the heavily mined channel, and into Mobile Bay, losing one monitor, USS *Tecumseh*, along the way. The fleet's progress was temporarily halted by the powerful Confederate ironclad CSS *Tennessee*, but the Union ships rammed and shelled her until she was forced to surrender. They then sank or captured all the remaining ships in the small Confederate squadron commanded by Admiral Franklin Buchanan, thus ending Mobile's role in the war.

Five months later, Admiral Porter had moved on Fort Fisher, which protected Wilmington, North Carolina, the remaining gap in the Federal blockade. His 59-ship fleet began its bombardment on January 13, 1865, while Union army soldiers established a beachhead. On the 15th, with the fleet firing point-blank, more than 2000 sailors and marines launched an amphibious assault while 3300 soldiers attacked from land. In the evening, the fort surrendered, and the Union had demonstrated again that it could strike wherever and whenever it wished.

Right: Union Admiral John Augustus Dahlgren, dubbed the 'Father of Naval Ordnance,' advocated mounting both light and heavy cannons of single calibers on warships rather than the many sizes then current. Dahlgren also designed smooth-bore guns that could fire explosive shells as well as shot. But these innovations were still not sufficient to overcome the radical improvement in protection represented by armorplating. During the war the ironclads were virtually impervious to naval gunfire. The old balance between offense and defense was restored only after the war when high-velocity rifled guns and armor-piercing shells were developed.

Left: Shot, shells, and torpedoes in front of the Confederate arsenal at Charleston. Torpedoes (mines) were designed to be anchored and were best suited to river warfare. They were used extensively by the Confederacy. Floating torpedoes were sometimes drifted down on a fleet in a river.

Above: USS *St. Louis*, the first of eight Union ironclads built by James Buchanan Eads, a steamboat engineer. It was built in 45 days, and its sister ships followed within the next 55 days. After the war, Eads oversaw construction of a steel bridge, still in use, over the Mississippi at St. Louis.

Right: Union gunners prepare a 9-inch Dahlgren gun for firing. Able to fire both shot and shell, this design, and an 11-inch version, became the basic naval ordnance of the 1850s. Early in the war 15-inch Dahlgrens were made specifically for the monitor ironclads, but an even larger gun for the next generation of ironclads was not produced.

Above left: USS *Monadnock*, built in 1864, was of a class of twin-turreted ironclads. It survived until 1874.

Above: John Ericsson, the designer and builder of the USS *Monitor*.

Left: The Confederate torpedo boat *David* aground at Charleston in 1865. Such a boat, with a 100-lb can of gunpowder fixed to the spar at the bow, could submerge its hull to reduce visibility. It would then run hard at the enemy, hoping that the right ship would be destroyed in the explosion. *David*-class boats had some successes. The only true submersible to see action, the hand-cranked CSS *Hunley*, sank in its only encounter.

Left: The iron-plated turret of the USS *Monitor*. The dents in the rotating turret near the empty gun port are from several of the 22 hits made by CSS *Virginia*. The gun is one of two 11-inch smooth-bore cannons. The famous duel between *Monitor* and *Virginia* (ex-*Merrimac*) did not, as some have claimed, introduce the world to the concept of ironclad warships. Both France and England had built armored ships in the 1850s. But the Battle of Hampton Roads was the first time such vessels were used in combat and thus marked a symbolic end to the 'Age of Fighting Sail.'

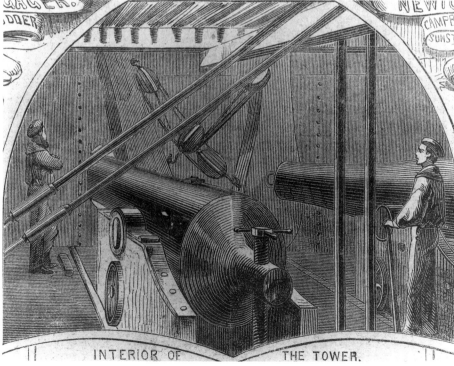

INTERIOR OF THE TOWER.

Above: March 9, 1862, the first encounter between ironclads. CSS *Virginia* and USS *Monitor* battled to a draw.

Left: The interior of the turret of *Monitor*, showing her 11-inch guns, one advanced for firing, the other behind a closed port for reloading.

PORT HUDSON.

Above: A Union river gunboat and steam frigate at the siege of Port Hudson, Louisiana. Hastily fortified by the Confederacy as a second stronghold on the Mississippi, Port Hudson surrendered on July 9, 1863, after the fall of Vicksburg.

Right: In a predawn battle that opened a stretch of the Mississippi River, a Federal flotilla disabled a smaller Confederate force near Memphis, Tennessee, on June 6, 1862. The Rebel force mustered only 28 guns to the Union's 68.

Left: *Chickamauga*, a lightly armed US Army transport, carried supplies along the Tennessee River.

Right: The Union gunboats *Mound City* and *Cincinnati* (background), part of a force of seven ironclads, were sunk in the Mississippi at Fort Pillow, Tenn., on May 10, 1862. The attacking squadron of eight Confederate gunboats was disabled and forced to withdraw to Memphis.

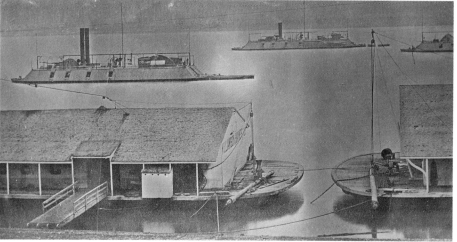

Above: During the Union attempt to establish control in Louisiana and Texas, the Federal fleet was hampered by low water on the Red River above Alexandria. On May 9, 1864, the gunboat *Lexington* passed thorugh a break in the dams built by Union engineers to raise the water level.

Right: Confederate ships attack the Union blockade at Galveston, Texas, on January 1, 1863.

Left: USS *Lexington* passes through one of the dams on the Red River and heads for the Mississippi, followed by the rest of the fleet.

Left below: Construction of the dams above the rapids on the Red River was completed in only 10 days.

Above: The port of Savannah, Georgia. In April 1862 the Union seized Fort Pulaski, 17 miles east of the city, and held it until the end of the war as part of the blockade of Savannah harbor.

Right: Cotton bales being loaded at a Southern port. During the war cottton production decreased by 80 percent, not only because of the blockade's effectiveness, but because the cotton land was needed for food crops.

Above: Union cavalry disembark near Port Royal, South Carolina. Capture of this port in November 1861 gave the blockading fleet a supply depot strategically located between the two major Confederate ports of Savannah and Charleston.

Above: The commerce raider CSS *Alabama* decoying merchant vessels toward herself by burning a prize.

Right: Captain John A. Winslow (third from left) poses with his officers on USS *Kearsarge* after destroying CSS *Alabama* off the coast of Cherbourg, France, June 19, 1864.

Left: Men of USS *Kearsarge* cheer as CSS *Alabama* settles in the water. A British steam yacht observing nearby picked up some survivors, including Captain Raphael Semmes, who escaped to England.

Left below: View of the spar-deck of USS *Hartford*, Farragut's flagship at the Battle of Mobile Bay. His victory on August 5, 1864, against the Rebel Ironclad ram *Tennessee* and a small fleet under Admiral Franklin Buchanan, effectively closed the Alabama port to blockade runners.

Above: Admiral David Glasgow Farragut standing in USS *Hartford*'s rigging as it brushes past Fort Morgan in Mobile Bay.

Right: A contemporary drawing of the Battle of Mobile Bay. As the Union fleet, protected by four monitors, enters Mobile Bay under the guns of Fort Morgan, ironclad *Tennessee* steams out to meet it.

Left: View from Fort Morgan, showing the top of the barracks and, in the distance, Union frigates and gunboats that had participated in the Battle of Mobile Bay.

Above: An engraving of the Battle of Mobile Bay. Here Farragut, in defiance of Rebel mines (known as 'torpedoes'), was said to exclaim, 'Damn the torpedoes, full speed ahead.'

The Decisive Campaigns (1864-1865)

'The Army of the Potomac is in splendid condition and evidently feels like whipping somebody,' wrote Grant, newly promoted to lieutenant general and given command of all the Federal armies. He planned personally to direct a move on Richmond now that the Confederacy had been seriously weakened by the Union victories of 1863; it would be Grant with 120,000 men against Lee with half that number. In a three-pronged assault, Grant would cut Lee off from Richmond with an attack across the Wilderness in northern Virginia; General Benjamin Butler would move along the south bank of the James; and General Franz Sigel would pressure Lee with raids in the Shenandoah Valley.

But Lee caught Grant in the Wilderness on May 5, 1864, halting his advance and costing him 17,000 men. Undaunted, Grant attempted to flank Lee to the southeast while drawing off Lee's cavalry under Jeb Stuart with his own troopers under Philip H. Sheridan. After a series of engagements, Stuart was killed at Yellow Tavern near Richmond on May 11.

For the next month Grant would repeatedly attack, be halted, then disengage and try once more to move between Lee and Richmond. The two armies met at Spotsylvania Court House (May 10-12), where Grant, having forced Lee to dig in, vowed 'to fight it out on this line if it takes all summer'; at North Anna River (May 23), where Lee split the Union army but was unable to follow his advantage; and at Cold Harbor (June 1-3), where terrible losses and no gains at last forced Grant to abandon his direct approach to Richmond.

He moved instead in Petersburg, an important rail junction south of Richmond. This time he actually succeeded in outmaneuvering Lee, but a hastily assembled force under P. G. T. Beauregard slowed the Union advance, and Lee was able to reinforce the city's defenses before the Union could press its fleeting advantage. Grant settled in to what would be a ten-month siege. Each side now counted half its force as casualties.

There were probes and stabs and even a spectacular attempt on the Confederate entrenchments that involved a long tunnel dug to the Rebel lines, at the end of which four tons of black powder were ignited. The Union attack in this Battle of the Crater (July 30) failed because of poor coordination of follow-up troops commanded by Ambrose E. Burnside. But Grant was content to wait, having finally pinned down Lee, the genius of mobile warfare.

On the same day, May 4, 1864, that Grant had headed south for Richmond, General William Tecumseh Sherman began to move 100,000 men of the armies of the Cumberland, the Ohio, and the Tennessee from Chattanooga toward the key city of Atlanta. Withdrawing before them were the 53,000 men of Joseph E. Johnston's Army of Tennessee. They would so slow Sherman that he would require two and a half months to march the 100 miles to the Georgia capital.

Repeatedly Sherman tried to flank Johnston, who fought only when pressed and avoided entrapment. At Kennesaw Mountain near Marietta, Georgia, Sherman forced Johnston to defend his railroad communications, but in three major uphill assaults on June 27, column after column of Federal troops were shot down as they reached the Confederate breastworks. The two forces each numbered about 17,000 men; the North had 2000 casualties, the South only 440.

Another Union setback had occurred earlier in the month when Sherman sent 8000 men under General S. D. Sturgis against Nathan Bedford Forrest. Awaiting the arrival on June 10 of the fatigued Federal troops at Brice's Crossroads in Mississippi, Forrest positioned his artillery and men to attack the Union flanks. The Federals broke, abandoning much of their equipment and their entire supply train.

On July 7 Johnston arrived outside Atlanta, but because Jefferson Davis considered him too cautious, he was replaced by the too-incautious John B. Hood. On July 20 Hood counterattacked, hitting hard at the Union Army of the Cumberland under George H. Thomas at Peachtree Creek. But Thomas, 'the Rock of Chickamauga,' held, and Hood withdrew to east of Atlanta. There, two days later, he failed to dislodge James B. McPherson's Union Army of the Tennessee, although McPherson himself was killed by Confederate skirmishers. Sherman then began what would be a four-week siege of Atlanta, choking off all rail lines into the city. On September 1 Hood evacuated Atlanta, destroying all the munitions and stores that he could not carry. Federal troops moved in the next morning.

Hood moved north in November, hoping to force Sherman to follow him out of Georgia into Tennessee. Sherman would not be drawn, but sent Thomas to check him. At Franklin, Tennessee, on November 30, a Union force under John M. Schofield turned back Confederate assaults and cost Hood 6000 men and five generals. Schofield, with Hood following closely, then moved on to Nashville, where Thomas was consolidating Federal forces. Hood took up a fortified position southeast of the city outside Thomas' ring of defenses. After what Grant considered unnecessary delays, Thomas attacked Hood's outnumbered Army of Tennessee on December 15, pushing it south. By the next day Hood's forces were shattered, and the Army of Tennessee would not fight a major battle again.

With Thomas engaging Hood, General Sherman moved to carry the war to the people of the South. Preparing for his march to the sea, Sherman destroyed anything in Atlanta that might be of use to the Confederacy, and then, in two wings, on November 16 he departed for Savannah with 60,000 men, 20 days' rations, and a determination to 'enforce a devastation more or less relentless.' He savaged the countryside with little opposition, and on December 21 occupied Savannah. To Lincoln he telegraphed, 'I beg to present you, as a Christmas gift, the city of Savannah . . . ,' and there he rested for a month while his army prepared for a campaign in the Carolinas.

On February 1, 1865, Sherman's army marched north into South Carolina, one wing pointed at Charleston and the other at Augusta. Smashing and burning what they could, the soldiers seemed to be wreaking vengeance on a state that they saw as the soul of the rebellion. Facing only the remnants of the now-reinstated Johnston's Army of Tennessee, the Union wings joined near Columbia, which surrendered without opposition on February 17. That night, a fire destroyed much of the town; though no one really knows how it started, the fire quickly became a symbol in the South of Sherman's ruthless march. Charleston was evacuated that same day by Confederate General William J. Hardee, and Fort Sumter, too, finally came into Union hands.

In the next four weeks, Sherman reached Bentonville, North Carolina, where Johnston mounted the last major assault on his advance. On April 14 Johnston at last surrendered near Raleigh. (On this day in Washington, Abraham Lincoln was shot; five days earlier, Grant had accepted Lee's surrender.)

While Grant was fighting his way out of the Wilderness and Sherman was marching to Atlanta, General Franz Sigel had been moving down the Shenandoah Valley with orders to sweep it clean of Rebels. But in June, Confederate General Jubal Early had moved his small army north through the valley toward the Potomac, putting into action a plan to make a feint attack on Washington. Driving back Sigel's forces at Harpers Ferry, he crossed into Maryland, easily taking Hagerstown and then routing a force under Lew Wallace at Frederick. On the afternoon of July 11, with the population of Washington thoroughly alarmed, Early entered the capital's northern outskirts, but with the arrival of Union reinforcements he was forced to withdraw to the Shenandoah Valley. Grant, from the first, had seen the feint for what it was and had not been fooled into diverting any of his troops from the siege of Petersburg.

In August, General Sheridan went into the Shenandoah, defeating Early at Winchester and Fisher's Hill in September. On October 19, when in his absence his army was surprised at Cedar Creek by an attack from Early's corps, Sheridan raced 21 miles to rally his men, who, despite heavy losses, went on to win a decisive battle. Then, moving east toward Petersburg in March 1865, Sheridan crushed Confederate defenses at Five Forks at the same time that Grant was launching a final, full-scale assault on Petersburg. On April 2 Lee abandoned that city; on the following day Richmond surrendered. By April 9 Meade and Sheridan had completely blocked the retreat of Lee's half-starved army, and, realizing the futility of further resistance, Lee requested a cease-fire. He and Grant met at the Virginia village of Appomattox Court House to work out surrender terms. Afterward Lee mounted his storied mare Traveller and returned to his men, whom he released from their duty. The bloodiest war in American history had at last ended.

Left: General Ulysses S. Grant at Cold Harbor, Virginia. Here Lee checked the Federal advance on Richmond in a battle (June 1-3) that cost the Union 12,000 casualties.

Above: Grant watches his men cross the James on their way to Petersburg in June 1864. For more than a month Lee had successfully foiled all his efforts to attack Richmond directly.

Left: Union soldiers wounded in the Battle of the Wilderness, May 5-6, try to escape Lee's furious attack. The Union losses were 17,600, more than double that of the Confederacy.

Above: Digging this canal at Dutch Gap was part of Benjamin Butler's scheme to bring Union gunboats to within firing range of Richmond's defenses. It failed.

Right: After being stalled by Lee in the Wilderness, Grant continued toward Richmond, his immediate goal being the crossroads at Spotsylvania. Here, on May 10-12, Lee's deeply entrenched troops failed to halt Grant's drive on Richmond. There were huge numbers of casualties on both sides.

Opposite: In the battle on the Orange Plank Road in the Wilderness Campaign, Confederate troops under Longstreet reinforce A. P. Hill's men to help check the Union advance on May 6.

Right: Artist Edwin Forbes penciled this scene of General Grant and his staff being greeted by his soldiers on the road from the Wilderness to Spotsylvania Court House.

Below: The grave of Confederate General Jeb Stuart at a Richmond cemetery in 1864. Mortally wounded at Yellow Tavern on May 11, he died in Richmond the next day at age 31.

Below right: Federal supplies being landed at the huge depot at City Point, Virginia. By mid-1864 the CSA was finding it ever more difficult to distribute its existing supplies.

Left: Seated on pews borrowed from a nearby church, the Union command was caught by photographer Timothy O'Sullivan as it prepared for the Battle of Cold Harbor. General Grant is at the left, leaning over the back of a pew. The costly and frustrating encounter at Cold Harbor would prompt Grant to change his tactics. He would abandon the plan of trying to attack Richmond directly and would instead attack its main supply center: Petersburg.

Above: A view of Petersburg, Virginia. For ten months – June 1864 to April 1865 – two armies confronted each other from a complex web of trenches. With Lee at last pinned down, Grant was content to wait.

Right: That Grant moved his forces so swiftly from Cold Harbor to the Petersburg front was due in part to some engineering feats such as this 2100-ft. pontoon bridge, built in half a day, to span the James River.

Above: A maze of fortified trenches slowly spread around Petersburg on both sides of the front, an ominous foreshadowing of the kind of war the world would experience in 1914-18.

Right: A Union deserter is hanged at Petersburg at the beginning of the siege. About 140 Union soldiers were executed for desertion during the war; many others were pardoned by Lincoln.

Right: At the headquarters of General Willcox outside Petersburg in August 1864, men pass the time with a cock fight.

Right below: Making gabions, rough baskets filled with earth and rocks, to be used in fortifications at the siege of Petersburg.

Left: Union infantry in the trenches surrounding besieged Petersburg in 1865.

Above: A blacksmith in the Union army at his portable field forge near Petersburg in August 1864.

Above: Confederate General Nathan Bedford Forrest. He was a successful businessman when he enlisted at 40, and he became a brilliant cavalry tactician. As Sherman headed for Atlanta, he detached a force to attack Forrest. On May 10, 1864, at Brice's Crossroads, Forrest's waiting Rebels outmaneuvered and then routed the superior Federal force.

Above: At Kennesaw Mountain near Marietta, Georgia, on June 27, Sherman forced Joseph E. Johnston's Rebels to stand and defend their rail communications. The well-entrenched Rebels repelled three uphill charges against their breastworks, causing 2000 casualties while losing only 440 of their own.

Right: A commemorative portrait of General Sherman celebrates his Atlanta campaign.

Opposite: General Sherman directs an artillery bombardment of Atlanta in August. General Hood evacuated the city on September 1 and Sherman entered the next day.

Left: Before Sherman's men left the city in November they tore up rails and destroyed anything else that could be of use to the Confederates.

Above: Peachtree Street in Atlanta. The destruction was a deliberate attempt by Sherman's departing troops to reduce the South's will and ability to conduct war.

Above: To prevent its use by Federal forces, this Atlanta railroad yard was destroyed by Rebel troops on September 1, before they evacuated the city.

Left: Rebel fortifications at Atlanta. Some of the lumber for the defenses was ripped from the homes in the rear.

Right: Union gun emplacements at the capitol in Nashville, Tennessee. General George Thomas fortified the city against an attack by Confederate John B. Hood encamped southeast of Nashville.

Right below: Hood had attempted to divert Sherman from his march to the sea by mounting a campaign far to his rear in Tennessee. Although Sherman did not pause in his march through Georgia, he did send General Thomas to Tennessee to deal with Hood. The armies met in an indecisive – though for Hood very costly – encounter at Franklin in November, and then Hood tried to besiege the Union army in Nashville. Shown here is part of the Federal defense line at Nashville.

Opposite: Thomas was prepared to let Hood exhaust himself in a protracted (and somewhat pointless) siege of Nashville, but the impatient Grant ordered the Union general to finish Hood off immediately. Thomas attacked on December 15, 1864, and within the next 48 hours he had shattered the Confederate Army of Tennessee.

Right: Union General William Tecumseh Sherman at Atlanta. His 37-day March to the Sea from Atlanta to Savannah with 60,000 men included a mandate to break the South's spirit. His men spread out along a 60-mile-wide front, systematically destroying property and industrial capacity.

Above: On December 20, before Sherman could cut off his escape, Confederate General Hardee took his army out of Savannah north toward South Carolina.

Left: Civilians, carrying what they can, flee before Sherman's army.

Below: As Sherman's force moved slowly toward the sea, railroad and telegraph lines were destroyed and the farms stripped of their produce.

Right: Burning the navy yard at Savannah to keep it from Northern hands.

Below right: Ruins of Columbia in central South Carolina after its occupation by Sherman's troops in February 1865. The burning of the city, perhaps wrongly attributed to the Union soldiers, became a symbol in the South of Northern cruelty.

Left A cartoon in *Frank Leslie's Illustrated Newspaper* depicts General Sherman as Santa Claus putting Savannah into Uncle Sam's stocking. On December 22, Sherman had telegraphed Lincoln, 'I beg to present you, as a Christmas gift, the city of Savannah. . . .'

Above: A pencil sketch, probably the work of William Waud, depicts a battle at Darbytown Road, Virginia, a small Union engagement on October 27, 1864, designed to cover a larger assault on Confederate lines at Petersburg.

Right: Alfred R. Waud's pencil sketch of Sheridan's ride. On October 19, 1864, Union General Philip Sheridan, who had been absent at a conference, learned that an attack by Jubal Early at Cedar Creek had panicked his men. He raced 21 miles to rally a counterattack and routed Early's force.

Far left: In July 1864 Confederate General Jubal Early launched a feint attack on Washington, but Grant was not deceived and diverted none of his troops from the Petersburg front.

Left: General George Armstrong Custer. After Jubal Early returned to the Shenandoah Valley from his foray into Washington, his army was much reduced by having to reinforce Lee at Richmond and Petersburg. On March 2, 1865, a Union cavalry force under Custer met Early's remaining force at Waynesboro and destroyed this last Rebel army in the Valley.

Right: A dramatic rendering of General Sheridan's celebrated ride. Rienzi, Sheridan's horse, was stuffed after his death and is now in Washington, D.C., in the Smithsonian Institution museum. Sheridan, who had risen from obscurity to become the Union army's premier cavalry commander, emerged from the war a hero. In time (1884) he would become the commander-in-chief of the United States Army.

Left: Engraving of Sheridan's troops moving up the Shenandoah Valley in December 1864. In March they crushed General Pickett's men at Five Forks, then joined Grant at Petersburg, where they helped block Lee's retreat from the besieged city.

Above: General Sheridan, seemingly all over the battlefield, led his force against Jubal Early's Confederates at Winchester on September 19, 1864. Pressed hard by Early's smaller force, Sheridan turned the enemy's flanks and forced its retreat.

Right: The 100-mile-long Shenandoah Valley was a haven for Confederate guerrillas such as John Singleton Mosby. Part of Sheridan's task was to clear them out. Here, in Edwin Forbes' drawing, a supply train is shown being recaptured from Mosby's raiders.

Right below: Alfred R. Waud sketched General George A. Custer and his staff on October 23, 1864, as they presented Confederate battle flags captured in the Valley.

Left: A romanticized night scene of a meeting of Colonel Mosby and his men at a pass in the Blue Ridge Mountains of Virginia.

Above: In October 1864, at Cedar Creek, General Sheridan ended organized Confederate resistance in the Valley.

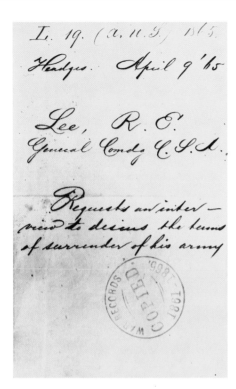

Above: The message sent by Lee to Grant on April 9, 1865, in which General Lee 'Requests an interview to discuss the terms of surrender of his army.'

Left: A photograph of Robert E. Lee by Mathew Brady, taken on April 20 at Lee's Richmond home shortly before he left to become president of Washington College (renamed Washington and Lee University after his death) in Lexington, Virginia.

Above: Richard Brooke's painting of battle-weary veterans furling the Stars and Bars of the Confederacy after the surrender. Many units hid their battle flags rather than give them up.

Right: General Lee's formal farewell to the men of the Army of Northern Virginia.

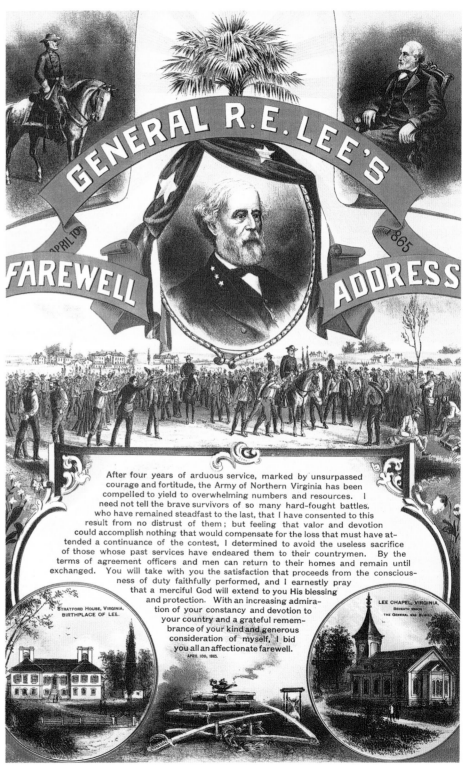

GENERAL R. E. LEE'S
FAREWELL ADDRESS
APRIL 10TH 1865

After four years of arduous service, marked by unsurpassed courage and fortitude, the Army of Northern Virginia has been compelled to yield to overwhelming numbers and resources. I need not tell the brave survivors of so many hard-fought battles, who have remained steadfast to the last, that I have consented to this result from no distrust of them; but feeling that valor and devotion could accomplish nothing that would compensate for the loss that must have attended a continuance of the contest, I determined to avoid the useless sacrifice of those whose past services have endeared them to their countrymen. By the terms of agreement officers and men can return to their homes and remain until exchanged. You will take with you the satisfaction that proceeds from the consciousness of duty faithfully performed, and I earnestly pray that a merciful God will extend to you His blessing and protection. With an increasing admiration of your constancy and devotion to your country and a grateful remembrance of your kind and generous consideration of myself, I bid you all an affectionate farewell.

APRIL 10th, 1865.

STRATFORD HOUSE, VIRGINIA,
BIRTHPLACE OF LEE.

LEE CHAPEL, VIRGINIA.
BENEATH WHICH
THE GENERAL WAS BURIED

Above: On the day before Lee's surrender, a visitor mourns beside a soldier's grave at a Union cemetery near Richmond.

Right: Remains of soldiers who fell at Cold Harbor being disinterred for reburial almost a year after that costly battle.

Above: The front page of *The New York Times* of April 10, 1865, announces the surrender of General Lee and his whole army.

Right: Union soldiers view the ruins of Richmond. On April 12, 1865, the principal business district was set afire by the evacuating defenders.

Above: Victory celebrations in the North after the surrender included the grand parade of the Army of the Potomac up Pennsylvania Avenue in Washington, D.C. on May 23, 1865.

Above right: A commemorative print of the final Union assault on Rebel siege lines at Petersburg.

Right: Burned-out streets of Richmond. With the aid of outside funding, the city was slowly rebuilt and many reminders of its proud heritage were restored.

Opposite: Soldiers and civilians abandon the Confederate capital to fires set in its mills, factories, and military arsenals.

Envoi

Although Lincoln had been elected as a minority president, his administration gained a solid Republican majority with the seating of the 37th Congress in July 1861. From 1862, however, Democrats controlled the politically powerful states of New York, Ohio, Illinois, Indiana, and Pennsylvania, and he faced rivals in his own party as well, particularly among those who supported the Radicals.

Lincoln strongly desired reelection, both for his own and for the national good as he saw it. But he faced the nominating convention with foreboding, concerned that military problems – the immense Union losses in the Wilderness and the slow progress against General Johnston in Georgia – and an accumulation of economic difficulties would hurt his chances.

Many disaffected Radicals found a potential candidate in Salmon P. Chase, the ambitious secretary of the treasury, but Lincoln's insistence on retaining Chase in the Cabinet left him unable to campaign actively. Another potential nominee was John C. Frémont, the explorer, soldier, and failed Republican presidential candidate of 1856. A council of extreme Radicals placed him in nomination, but he withdrew his name. Lincoln's nomination, however, was not really in doubt. He was an experienced and wily politician who had his deputies working aggressively to secure the state delegations for him and who exploited arriving news of Union victories for his cause. The Republican convention met in Baltimore on June 7, 1864, and nominated him (unanimously) its candidate for president; for vice president it chose Andrew Johnson, a War Democrat from Tennessee, in an effort to balance the ticket.

The Democratic convention on August 29 nominated the popular General George B. McClellan. His poor performance as Union commander he attributed to Lincoln, claiming that the president had wished to disgrace him. He ran on a 'peace' platform that called the Republicans' prosecution of the war a failure and demanded an immediate end to hostilities and a convention to negotiate peace with the secessionist states. General Sherman's timely capture of Atlanta, Farragut's victories in Mobile Bay, and Sheridan's successes in the Shenandoah Campaign became testaments to Lincoln's ability to prosecute the war to a satisfactory conclusion. McClellan received only 21 electoral votes – those of Delaware, New Jersey, and Kentucky. Lincoln received 212 electoral votes and a 408,000 popular majority out of 4,019,000 votes cast.

This vote of confidence virtually eliminated opposition, and Lincoln was able to give prominence to his lenient plans for reunion. In his second inaugural address he uttered eloquently a call for a peace 'With malice toward none; with charity for all.' He would live long enough to see the surrender of the principal army of the Confederacy, but not to implement his wishes for a new South.

On April 14, 1865, General Robert Anderson raised over Fort Sumter the flag he had lowered four years before. That evening, President and Mrs. Lincoln attended a play – *Our American Cousin* – at Ford's Theater in Washington. Approaching from behind, a young actor, John Wilkes Booth, fired one shot from his derringer into Lincoln's brain. The president died the next morning, with his son Robert, Cabinet members, and others keeping vigil by his bed. Andrew Johnson took the oath of office before noon.

John Wilkes Booth, one of ten children of famed Shakespearean actor Junius Brutus Booth, was zealously pro-Confederate. He and co-conspirators had already twice failed in plots to kidnap and ransom the president, but after Lee's surrender they apparently decided that Lincoln's death, as well as the deaths of other government officials, would better serve the South.

After shooting Lincoln, Booth leaped to the stage, breaking a leg, and escaped out a side door. With David Herold he rode to Maryland. His leg had been set by Dr. Samuel Mudd, who would claim that he did not know Booth and knew nothing of the assassination attempt. Meanwhile, another conspirator, Lewis Payne, inflicted several knife wounds on the face and neck of Secretary of State William Seward, who was in bed recuperating from an accident. Secretary of War Edwin Stanton directed the search for the conspirators, and on April 26 Booth and Herold were discovered in a tobacco barn near Bowling Green, Virginia. Booth refused to surrender and was shot, perhaps by his own hand. Eight people were seized and charged with conspiring to assassinate Lincoln, Johnson, Seward, and Stanton. Four were tried and hanged; three, including Dr. Mudd, received life sentences; one received a six-year sentence. Of those serving sentences, one died of yellow fever and three, including Mudd, were pardoned by Johnson in 1869.

Andrew Johnson was if anything more conciliatory than Lincoln in addressing the problems of Reconstruction – the political process of restoring normal relations with the Southern states and reintegrating them into the Union. The process had been started in the middle of the war. Lincoln hoped that some reintegration could begin as areas were cleared of Confederate troops, and he announced in December 1863 that he would regard a state as restored to the Union if one-tenth of the number of citizens who had voted in 1860 established a new state government and abolished slavery. There was, however, considerable controversy in the Congress over how the new state governments should be recognized and over how much of a role the executive branch should play. New constitutions were framed in several states – Louisiana, Arkansas, Tennessee – but Congress refused to recognize their votes in the election of 1864, and their congressmen were not seated.

After Lincoln's death, Johnson appointed provisional governors in the former Confederate states. They summoned conventions that were required to repeal secession, abolish slavery, and pledge to support the U.S. Constitution. By the end of the year ten new governments were in place, and the 13th Amendment, abolishing slavery, had been adopted. But the Southern states had failed to enfranchise the former slaves and had elected numbers of prominent Confederates to governmental office.

Outraged by the effects of Johnson's leniency – the seeming compromise of the victory on the battlefields – the Radicals, who had increased their strength in Congress in the 1866 election, passed a series of Reconstruction Acts that had the effect of reversing the Lincoln-Johnson program. The states were reorganized under military authority. The officers in command ordered new state constitutional conventions and new elections for both state and federal offices. Ratification of the 14th Amendment was made a requirement for readmission, which not only gave all the rights of citizens to blacks, but disenfranchised the former white office holders.

Conservative white Southerners looked to Johnson for help, and he tried, within his limited powers, to support them. But Congressional Republicans impeached him in 1868, and though he survived by one vote, he accepted his inability to fight the Radicals. By 1870 all of the former states of the Confederacy were back in the Union, the majority under governments dominated by Radical Republican machines. Although corrupt and wasteful, the 'carpetbag' politicians did effect some meaningful reforms, such as in providing public services and improving legal processes. But by the mid-1870s the scandals of machine politics had alienated public support in both the North and South, and conservative Democratic governments began to reappear. But if the quality of government improved, the status of blacks did not. By the turn of the century blacks in the Deep South were still finding it extremely difficult to exercise their civil and economic rights and, indeed, had been virtually disenfranchised by stratagems such as literacy tests and poll taxes. Not for more than another half century would federal institutions actively support legal challenges to white preeminence.

Right: President Lincoln's second inauguration. Before taking the oath of office from Salmon P. Chase, now chief justice, Lincoln spoke of his hope that the war would soon be over, and then he exhorted his audience: 'With malice toward none; with charity for all; with firmness in the right, let us strive on to finish the work we are in; to bind up the nation's wounds . . . to do all which may achieve a just, and a lasting peace, among ourselves, and with all nations.'

LITTLE MAC, IN HIS GREAT TWO HORSE ACT, IN THE PRESIDENTIAL CANVASS OF 1864.

Left: Political cartoon published during the 1864 presidential campaign, showing Lincoln's challenger, George B. McClellan, attempting to ride two hores – war and peace – at the same time.

Below: On November 8, 1864, election day in the Union, soldiers of the Army of the Potomac went to the polls and gave their overwhelming support to President Lincoln.

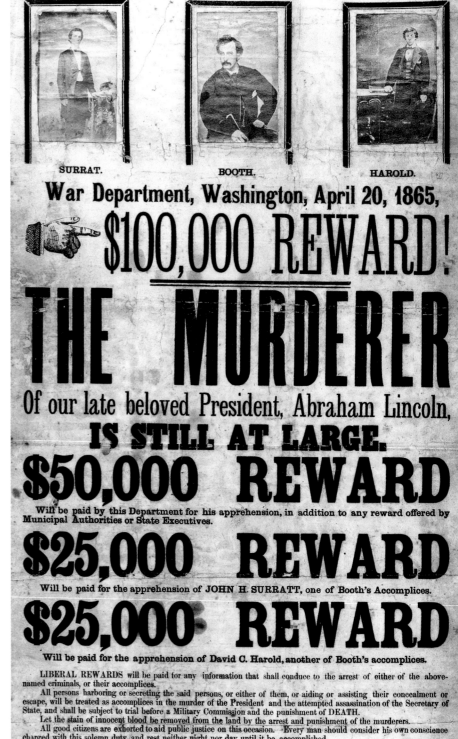

Above: In a somewhat belatedly-printed illustration of the event on the evening of April 14, 1865, John Wilkes Booth, having shot the President and stabbed one of his guests, Major Henry Rathbone, leaps from Lincoln's box at Ford's Theater. Booth caught his spur on the drapery and broke a leg as he fell to the stage shouting (by some accounts), *'Sic semper tyrannus!'* (Thus ever to tyrants). He escaped through a side door and rode off into the night.

Right: Secretary of War Edwin M. Stanton declared martial law in Washington and directed a wide-ranging manhunt for Booth and his co-conspirators. Meanwhile, Booth had his leg set at the home of Dr. Samuel A. Mudd in Maryland, then made his way south to Virginia, with the aid of David Herold. There Union soldiers discovered them hiding in a tobacco barn. Booth refused to surrender, the barn was set afire, and Booth was shot, perhaps by himself.

Left: After lying in state in the Capitol, Lincoln's body was placed aboard a funeral train for Springfield, Illinois, on April 21. Here his hearse passes through Chicago on May 1. He was buried at Oak Ridge Cemetery in Springfield.

Far left below: On July 7 four of the conspirators were hanged: Mary Surratt, David Herold, George Atzerodt, and Lewis Payne. Four others, including Dr. Mudd, had received prison sentences.

Left below: John Wilkes Booth, a good Shakespearean actor, was violently pro-Confederate, and his kidnapping plots were already known to the War Department before his assassination attempt.

Right: Reconstruction governments sent a number of blacks to the U.S. Congress, including (left to right) Senator Hiram R. Revels (Miss.) and Representatives Benjamin S. Turner (Ala.), Robert C. De Large (S.C.), Josiah T. Walls (Fla.), Jefferson H. Long (Ga.), Joseph H. Rainy (S.C.), and R. Brown Elliot (S.C.).

Below: A cartoon in *Puck* depicts the 'strong' Republican carpetbag state governments imposing their will on the South until the mid-1870s, and the 'weak' conservative Democratic governments that followed.

Died,

NEAR THE SOUTH-SIDE RAIL ROAD,

ON SUNDAY, APRIL 9th, 1865,

The Southern Confederacy,

AGED FOUR YEARS.

CONCEIVED IN SIN, BORN IN INIQUITY, NURTURED BY TYRANNY, DIED OF A CHRONIC ATTACK OF PUNCH.

ABRAHAM LINCOLN, Attending Physician.

U. S. GRANT, Undertaker.

JEFF DAVIS, Chief Mourner.

EPITAPH.

Gentle stranger, drop a tear,
The C. S. A. lies buried here;
In youth it lived and prosper'd well,
But like Lucifer it fell;
Its body here, its soul in — well
E'en if I knew I wouldn't tell.

Rest C. S. A., from every strife,
Your death is better than your life;
And this one line shall grace your grave—
Your death gave freedom to the slave.

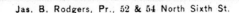

Jas. B. Rodgers, Pr., 52 & 54 North Sixth St.

Opposite right below: A sketch for a Thomas Nast cartoon for *Harper's Weekly* of December 31, 1864, portrayed the elements of Lincoln's Reconstruction policy. He invites the defeated Jefferson Davis and Robert E. Lee to seats at a banquet welcoming back the Confederate states.

Left: A handbill published in the North following Lee's surrender at Appomattox celebrates the demise of the CSA. The regional animosities bred by the war persisted for many years, sometimes fueled by the harsh Reconstruction policies urged by vindictive radical Republicans. In 1877 Federal troops were finally recalled from Louisiana, the last Southern state still to be governed under Northern supervision. In a sense, this, too, marked an end to the agonizing period in American history which began when the first cannonball struck Fort Sumter.

THE TWO PRESIDENTS.

PRESIDENT ANDY—"Hullo, Jeff, how is your trial getting on?"
PRESIDENT JEFF—"I've just got a respite for a month or two!"
PRESIDENT ANDY—"You're a lucky dog, Jeff—I'm being tried all the time."

1868

Acknowledgments

The publisher would like to thank the following people who helped in the preparation of this book: Adrian Hodgkins, who designed it; Rita Longabucco, who did the picture research; Florence Norton, who prepared the index; and John Kirk, who edited the text.

Picture Credits

All photographs courtesy Library of Congress and the National Archives.

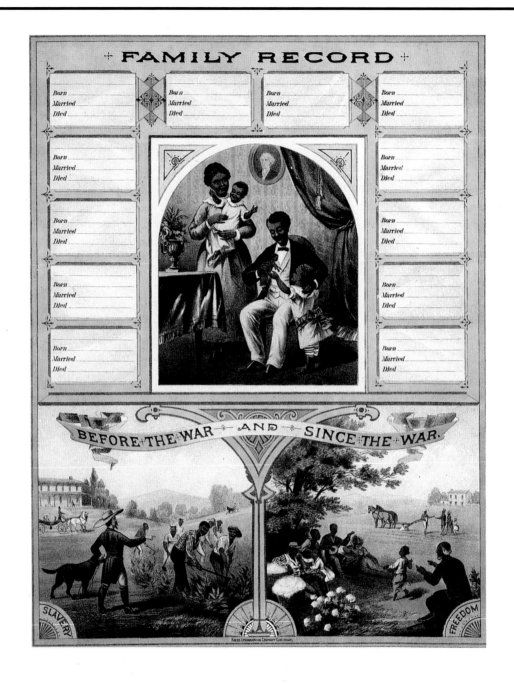